EDWARD STUART TALBOT
AND
CHARLES GORE

THE BISHOP AND MRS. TALBOT AT THEIR
GOLDEN WEDDING

Photograph by Russell & Sons

EDWARD STUART TALBOT

AND

CHARLES GORE

Witnesses to and Interpreters of the
Christian Faith in Church and State

ALBERT MANSBRIDGE

C.H., Hon. M.A. (Oxon.), Hon. LL.D. (Cambridge,
Manchester, and Pittsburg)

With a Foreword by
THE ARCHBISHOP OF YORK

London
J. M. DENT AND SONS LIMITED

TO
JAMES BUCHANAN SEATON
BISHOP OF WAKEFIELD
SOMETIME PRINCIPAL OF CUDDESDON
AND
ERIC GRAHAM
PRINCIPAL OF CUDDESDON

PREFATORY NOTE

THE three lectures contained in this book were delivered at Cuddesdon College, Oxford, during 1934, as the witness of a layman who, for over forty years, was inspired, advised, and helped in all his work by Edward Stuart Talbot and Charles Gore.

It is hoped that they will serve as preludes to, and increase interest in, the official biographies which are now in course of preparation.

A full-length biography of Bishop Talbot by Lady Stephenson is expected from the S.P.C.K. in the summer of 1935, and of Bishop Gore by the Rev. Dr. Leonard Prestige from Messrs. Heinemann in the near future.

October 1934.   A. M.

THE author wishes to express his thanks to Mrs. Lionel Ford, the Rev. L. C. Green-Wilkinson, the Rev. J. Grimes, Mr. and Mrs. Christopher Turnor, King's College, London, the Trustees of the National Portrait Gallery, Messrs. Bassano, the National Magazine Company, and Messrs. Russell and Sons, Southsea, for permission to reproduce portraits or photographs, and to the Dean of Westminster for his sketches.

THE author's royalties on this book will be devoted to the funds of the Church Tutorial Classes Association, of which Bishop Gore, in the Preface to *Students and the Faith*, a history of the Association's first ten years of life, spoke the following words: 'Every servant of the truth—every believer in the gospel—must wish the Association a measure of success in its great enterprise of which we see at present only the earliest promise.'

CONTENTS

LIST OF ILLUSTRATIONS

CHRONOLOGY

	Bishop Talbot	Bishop Gore	Outstanding Events in Church and State
1833			Keble's Sermon on National Apostasy.
1844	Born (Feb. 19th). Son of the Hon. John Chetwynd Talbot and Caroline, daughter of the Earl of Wharncliffe.		
1845			Newman seceded to Rome.
1852	Death of the Hon. J. C. Talbot.		
1853		Born (Jan. 22nd). Son of the Hon. Charles Gore and Augusta Countess of Kerry.	
1854			Outbreak of Crimean War.
1857			Indian Mutiny.
1859			Darwin's *Origin of Species* published.
1860			English Church Union founded. *Essays and Reviews* published.
1861			Victor Emmanuel proclaimed King of Italy. Outbreak of Civil War in the United States.
1862	Entered Christ Church, Oxford.	Entered May Place, Malvern (Prep. School).	

ix

	Bishop Talbot	Bishop Gore	Outstanding Events in Church and State
1866	Awarded 1st Class in the Hon. School of Literae Humaniores, 1st Class in Hon. School of Law and Modern History, and Ellerton Theological Essay Prize. Subject: 'The Influence of Christianity on Slavery.' Elected Senior Student of Christ Church, Oxford.	Entered Harrow	Excommunication of Bishop Colenso. Death of John Keble. Seeley's *Ecce Homo* published.
1867	Appointed Tutor in Modern History at Christ Church, Oxford.		Second Reform Act. Commission on Ritual appointed. First Pan-Anglican Conference at Lambeth.
1868			Archibald Campbell Tait translated to Archbishopric of Canterbury. Foundation stone of Keble College laid.
1869	Ordained Deacon by Bishop Samuel Wilberforce.	Confirmed at Harrow.	
1870	Ordained Priest by Bishop Mackarness. Married the Hon. Lavinia Lyttelton. Appointed Warden of Keble College, Oxford.	Won Open Scholarship at Balliol College, Oxford.	Outbreak of Franco-Prussian War. Decree of Papal Infallibility promulgated.
1871			Abolition of University Tests.
1875		Awarded 1st Class in the Honours School of Literae Humaniores.	

Bishop Talbot	*Bishop Gore*	*Outstanding Events in Church and State*
	Elected Fellow of Trinity College, Oxford.	
1876	Ordained Deacon by Bishop Mackarness. Curate at Christ Church, Bootle. Curate at St. Margaret's, Princes Road, Liverpool.	
1878	Ordained Priest by Bishop Mackarness.	Second Pan-Anglican Conference.
1880	Appointed Vice-principal of Cuddesdon. Christian Social Union founded.	
1881		Revised Version of New Testament published. Oxford Mission to Calcutta opened first Mission House.
1882	Chaplain to the Archbishop of Canterbury.	Death of Edward Bouverie Pusey
1883	Visited Oxford Mission to Calcutta.	E. W. Benson translated to Archbishopric of Canterbury.
1884	Appointed Principal of the Pusey House.	
1885		Third Reform Act passed. Revised Version of Old Testament published.
1887	Society of the Resurrection formed.	

	Bishop Talbot	Bishop Gore	Outstanding Events in Church and State
1888			Third Pan-Anglican Conference.
1889	Proceeded B.D. and D.D. (Oxon). Appointed Vicar of Leeds and Canon of Ripon. 'The Preparation in History for Christ' (chapter 4 in *Lux Mundi*).	(ed.) *Lux Mundi*. 'The Holy Spirit and Inspiration' (chapter 8 in *Lux Mundi*).	London Dock Strike.
1890		Visited Oxford Mission to Calcutta.	Trial of Bishop King.
1891		Delivered Bampton Lectures on *The Incarnation of the Son of God*. *The Mission of the Church*.	
1893		Appointed Vicar of Radley, Oxford. Senior of the Community of the Resurrection.	
1894	Chaplain in Ordinary to Queen Victoria.	Appointed Canon of Westminster.	
1895	Consecrated Bishop of Rochester. *Some Titles and Aspects of the Eucharist*. *Leeds Parish Church Sermons 1889–95*.	Became Hon. Fellow of Trinity College, Oxford.	
1896		Hon. D.D. conferred by Edinburgh University. *Exposition of the Sermon on the Mount*.	Frederick Temple translated to the Archbishopric of Canterbury. Fourth Pan-Anglican Conference.
1898		Hon. Chaplain to Queen Victoria.	

	Bishop Talbot	*Bishop Gore*	*Outstanding Events in Church and State*
		Exposition of Epistle to the Ephesians. Prayer and the Lord's Prayer.	
1899		Appointed Lecturer in Pastoral Theology at Cambridge. Exposition of Epistle to the Romans.	Outbreak of Boer War.
1900		Chaplain in Ordinary to Queen Victoria.	
1901		Chaplain in ordinary to King Edward VII. Proceeded D.D. (Oxon). The Body of Christ.	Death of Queen Victoria.
1902		Consecrated Bishop of Worcester.	
1903			Randall Davidson translated to the Archbishopric of Canterbury.
1904		Hon. D.C.L. conferred by Oxford University.	
1905	Translated to the See of Southwark. Southwark Sermons.	Translated to the See of Birmingham.	
1908	Hon. LL.D. conferred by Cambridge University.		Fifth Pan-Anglican Conference.
1909	The Fullness of Christ.	Hon. LL.D. conferred by Cambridge University. Hon. LL.D. conferred by Birmingham University.	
1910			International Missionary Conference at Edinburgh.

	Bishop Talbot	Bishop Gore	Outstanding Events in Church and State
1911	Translated to the See of Winchester.	Translated to the See of Oxford.	
1914			Outbreak of Great War.
1916		*The Religion of the Church.*	National Mission of Repentance and Hope.
1917	Chairman of Commission on 'The Army and Religion.'		
1918		*Dominant Ideas and Corrective Principles.*	Armistice signed.
1919	*Spiritual Sanctions of The League of Nations*	Resigned Bishopric of Oxford. Appointed Lecturer in Theology at King's College, London. Hon. D.D. conferred by Durham University.	Enabling Act passed. Versailles Peace Treaty signed.
1920	Conducted quiet day preceding Lambeth Conference.	*Exposition of the Epistles of St. John.*	Sixth Pan-Anglican Conference—Appeal to all Christian Peoples.
1921		*Christian Moral Principles.*	
1922		Became Hon. Fellow of Balliol College, Oxford, and Hon. Fellow and Life Governor of King's College, London.	
1923	Resigned bishopric of Winchester.	Took part in third Malines Conversations.	Prayer Book Measure given general approval by Church Assembly.
1924		Became Dean of the Theological Faculty of King's College, London. Visited Egypt, the	

There are few names that stand higher in the esteem and affection of countless friends than that of EDWARD STUART TALBOT, whose Episcopate lasted for twenty-eight years, and comprised in succession the Sees of Rochester, Southwark, and Winchester. These friends, we know full well, are eager to erect some permanent Memorial of his great work. A representative Committee have unanimously agreed to the following scheme, which is of a twofold nature.

1. It is proposed to place a recumbent Statue of the Bishop on the south side of the Sanctuary of Southwark Cathedral, near to that of another great Bishop of Winchester, Lancelot Andrewes. Mr. Cecil Thomas, A.R.B.S., who designed Archbishop Davidson's Monument in Canterbury Cathedral, has been commissioned to carry out the work.

2. It is also proposed, as part of the Memorial, that a Church closely associated with Bishop Talbot's name shall be elected at Mottingham, a large new building area in the diocese of Southwark.

To carry out the full scheme at least Twelve Thousand Pounds will be required, but we are confident that both these proposals will make a strong appeal to all friends of Edward Talbot, and we ask for the support not only of his own personal circle, but also of that vastly wider public who felt his influence and power.

The Hon. Treasurer of the Fund is the Marquis of Salisbury, and contributions should be addressed to the Westminster Bank, Ltd., 1 St. James's Square, S.W.1, and Cheques and other remittances made payable to ' The Talbot Memorial Fund." We venture to hope that contributions and promises may be sent in as soon as possible.

Bishop Talbot	Bishop Gore	Outstanding Events in Church and State
	Sudan, Palestine, and Syria. Hon. D.Phil. conferred by University of Athens. *The Reconstruction of Belief* (issued in 3 vols. 1921–4 as *Belief in God, Belief in Christ, The Holy Spirit and the Church.*)	
1925		Universal Conference on Faith and Work.
1926	*Can We then Believe?*	
1927		Prayer Book Measure rejected by Parliament. Lausanne Conference on Faith and Order.
1928	*Christ and Society.*	Second Prayer Book Measure rejected by Parliament. Cosmo Gordon Lang translated to Archbishopric of Canterbury.
1929	Delivered Gifford Lectures at St. Andrews on *The Philosophy of the Good Life.* *Jesus of Nazareth.* (ed.) *New Commentary on Holy Scripture.*	
1930	Conducted retreat before Lambeth Conference.	Seventh Pan-Anglican Conference.
1931	Visit to India.	
1932	*Reflections on the Litany.*	
1934 Died (Jan. 30th).	Died (Jan. 17th).	

EDWARD STUART TALBOT

1844–1934

Warden of Keble College	.	1870–88
Vicar of Leeds	. .	1889–95
Bishop of Rochester .	.	1895–1905
Bishop of Southwark	.	1905–11
Bishop of Winchester	.	1911–23

EDWARD STUART TALBOT stood high among the men
of his time through his combination of sound learning
and great administrative ability with the gift of radiant
happiness and the questing mind of a child. He was
powerful in all his ways, but he won the hearts of men
by the magnetism of an unfailing humility. He rejoiced
in all the little happenings and simple things of a life
which was largely fulfilled in high and great places.

His backbone was *moral*—he was deficient (*how* he knew it)
mystically—and he seemed lacking also on the *other-worldly side*—
perhaps this was part of his delicious, sane, vital, interested, loving
this-worldliness. But he had more of a hold upon the unseen than
he knew or allowed—a very real saintliness—and spiritual grandeur.

He loved and rejoiced openly in all things which were
natural, simple, and pure. His interest and enthusiasm
lit up a countenance which was inexpressibly beautiful
in its gentleness. He sorrowed with men even as he
was ever ready to rejoice.

During his last years these characteristics deepened.
They dominated his being. Lame and increasingly
deaf as he was, he steadily pursued his way. Nothing
daunted him; he would miss no event. He was happy
and active even to the end of his earthly life. Courageously questing, he passed the portals of this world with
his 'face in ripe age,' 'as the bright light upon the
holy candlestick.'

Born on February 19th 1844, Edward Stuart Talbot was the second son of the Hon. John Chetwynd Talbot and Caroline, daughter of the first Lord Wharncliffe. The Talbot family traces its ancestry back to the Middle Ages, and he was thus the inheritor of a great tradition. His own parents were deeply religious and they created a home life which inspired the boy and gave him standards and patterns enduring in type. Sorrow fell upon the family all too soon. Edward was barely eight years old when his father died. Yet he was fortunate in having a wise brother John,[1] nine years his senior, and a saintly mother who lived tranquilly in the spirit of the early Tractarians, and who secured one of its wise and devoted sons—Robert Shapland Hunt— as Vicar of the little parish of Mark Beech in which the Talbot home was set.

His schooldays, passed first at Geddington under a vicar tutor, then at Charterhouse, were ended prematurely by an illness which continued for some three years. In spite of this handicap the foundations of his later scholarship were well laid. As a day-boy at Charterhouse he had his admiration aroused by two remarkable 'gown boys' at the head of the School, Henry Nettleship and R. C. Jebb, who later filled Classical Chairs, the one at Oxford and the other at Cambridge. With Talbot, admiration ever beckoned to emulation.

The schoolboy found a welcome in two 'second homes,' Hawarden and Hagley, whose heads, William Ewart Gladstone and Lord Lyttelton, he venerated as Christian heroes. In their families he found the fellowship he needed in the comparative loneliness of his own life. Hagley, indeed, bestowed upon him later a supreme gift in his wife, a loved companion, a pattern and ensample.

After his recovery from his illness, he entered Christ Church in October 1862, and worked there, under

[1] Born 1835, died 1910. M.P. for West Kent, and later for the University of Oxford. Privy Councillor.

G. W. Kitchin [1] and Henry Thompson,[2] with the patience, skill and eagerness which were characteristic of him. He gained first classes in the final Classical School and in the old School of Law and Modern History. There followed four quiet, busy years as Senior Student of Christ Church and Tutor in Modern History. Dr. Pusey described him at this time as 'chivalrous, devoted, enthusiastic, and gifted with high talents.'

Christ Church was traditionally ecclesiastical, and it was also characteristically conservative and old-world. It stood largely aloof from the newer intellectual influences which had their centre at Balliol. To Talbot this was a definite advantage. It strengthened and deepened his Christian moral anchorage, the result of that Tractarian piety which pulsed in his being, and at the same time, without destroying his natural sympathy and open-mindedness, it taught him a certain critical detachment towards some of the more extreme intellectual fashions of his time. Thus it was that, while perplexed at the 'prevailing intellectual tone of the University' which apparently went counter to the things which he had been taught to value, he was fit and ready to make common cause with such men as J. B. Mozley,[3] Henry Scott Holland,[4] R. C. Moberly,[5] and, a little later, Charles Gore. Together they made a forceful company in which Talbot joyously served and in its ranks fought powerfully and victoriously for the Faith.

In 1868 the first stone of Keble College was laid. Erected as a memorial to John Keble, it was to be a

[1] George William Kitchin (1827–1912). Tutor of Christ Church, Oxford, 1852–83, Dean of Winchester 1883–94, Dean of Durham 1894–1912.

[2] Henry Louis Thompson, Student of Christ Church, Oxford, 1858–78.

[3] James Bowling Mozley (1813–78). Regius Professor of Divinity at Oxford 1871–8.

[4] Henry Scott Holland (1847–1918). Balliol, Oxford, 1866–70, Senior Student of Christ Church 1870–82, Canon of St. Paul's 1884–1910, Regius Professor of Divinity at Oxford 1910–18.

[5] Robert Campbell Moberly (1845–1903). New College, Oxford, 1863–7, Senior Student of Christ Church 1867–80, Regius Professor of Pastoral Theology at Oxford 1892–1903.

Church College, accessible to men of small means, most of whom were seeking ordination. Henry Parry Liddon [1] was the obvious Warden, but he, feeling that the claims of the office would hinder his own special work, felt compelled to refuse. Talbot was offered the Wardenship and accepted. At the time he had just been ordained to the Priesthood and was contemplating marriage.

Conventional Oxford feeling was critical, if not hostile. The creation of a sectarian college after the abolition of the Tests appeared to be an attempt to get back in spirit, if not in fact, to an older and rejected order of things.

The peculiar difficulties which the new College and its young untried Warden had to face can only be estimated by an Oxford man of the time. One such, himself a Bishop, has placed the thoughts which occurred to him, as he recalled those early days, at our disposal:

You might fairly emphasize the wonderful wisdom with which he guided Keble in the early days. It started, didn't it, in 1870? and I went up to Christ Church in 1872! I can remember a caricature of 'the Keble Eight' in a shop window in the Broad. The crew were all in cassocks, and the Coxswain (Talbot) in vestments! That, of course, was silly, but it just showed what might have been in people's minds. Clearly, Keble had to be 'Church,' and it had to be 'economical.' But yet it had to be *in* Oxford and *of* Oxford; not wholly severed from the life, let us say, of Christ Church, nor from the good that had sometimes got mixed up with expensive ways! It must be at once *like* and *unlike* the rest of Oxford. It must have a touch of distinction not sought or strained after or sprinkled on the top of it; but natural to it and in its veins.

This, I think, the Talbot, Lyttelton, Gladstone connection, with all its ramifications, helped to supply, and it was personified in the Warden. With all his humility Talbot was, after all (he couldn't help it), rather 'magnificent'! He claimed as you know, yes, and got, the help of all sorts of good tutors and lecturers; great people came and spent week-ends, and it was a sort of honour to be invited to the Warden's house!

They were not deliberately imported! They were the sort of people he knew, the sort of people who would naturally come to see him, and learn how he was getting on.

[1] Henry Parry Liddon (1829–90). Vice-Principal of Cuddesdon 1854–9, Vice-Principal of St. Edmund's Hall 1859–70, Dean Ireland's Professor of Exegesis 1870–82, Canon of St. Paul's 1870–90.

The alternatives of making Keble just like any other place, and of making it fatally different were fairly open to him; and the latter would, perhaps, have been the easiest, but had he chosen it I don't think that Keble would have done so well.

Keble became a social and intellectual centre in which Gladstone and the circle at Hawarden were frequent visitors. It formed, as it were, a sort of counter-poise to that other brilliant group which Jowett gathered round him at Balliol. It was a fortunate circumstance that Hawarden kept the Warden and his wife in touch with big people at their noblest.

Talbot's years at Keble were fruitful. We may imagine him, prior to 1870, eager, conscientious, keen, but taking life very seriously, regarding it as a long and hard, perhaps lonely, journey. Then there entered into it the joyous presence of Lavinia Lyttelton, who became his wife in 1870. She had the great gifts of humour and common sense. Through her constant encouragement Talbot was lifted out of himself. She widened the circle of friends in which he moved, so that he was enabled to draw the best from the social life and culture of his time. She gave an absolute sparkle to the Keble days.

A new world opened around him. To the happiness of his home was added the satisfaction of seeing the College developing in influence and strength. The fear that the College would be neglected and without influence was soon dissipated, and it became for many an Oxford centre, and exercise the power for good which its founders had hoped and prayed for.

The memories of Talbot at Keble are altogether delightful. Humour went hand in hand with admonition. 'In Lent,' he remarked to an undergraduate, 'we provide fish for those who wish to fast, and meat for those who do not, but I observe that you help yourself to both!'

The foundation of Lady Margaret Hall in 1878, largely due to his efforts and wisdom, delighted him greatly.

As one of a notable company of theologians, he helped

to develop the high ideals, profound scholarship, and lofty thought which made Oxford in the 'eighties the source of the movement which found expression in *Lux Mundi*. With it went, to use his own words, 'new developments of Christian activity in the Church's name.'

Talbot was never a prolific writer, but in spite of the difficulties and problems of the new college, he found time for intensive thinking and discussion, the results of which may be found in his *Lux Mundi* essay on 'The Preparation in History for Christ.'

Evidence of a line of thought to which he ever adhered throughout his long life is to be found in a private paper written in 1883 :

A Catholic Theology utterly fixed in its great central principles and in many of their corollaries, yet ever yielding up new meanings, even from its central depths, in the light of other knowledge and human development—such a theology, and at the same time a Church system, unchanging in one sense yet elastic in another— and these two together capable of laying hold upon the future, its movements, questions, temptations, advantages, discoveries, this is what we want.

He was throughout life a 'strong man with a wonderful constitution—never hot and never cold—always sleeping well and with not a nerve in his make-up,' yet he was much hindered during these years by attacks of periostitis—inflammation of the lining of the bone. This was not properly treated in 1884, the doctors delayed an operation on his left leg until too late, and he came very near death. If it had not been for the wonderful spirit and courage of Mrs. Talbot, who always regarded 'difficulties as an inspiration to higher effort,' he might never have returned to active life. The illness left him with a permanently lame leg, but he conquered the disability to such an extent that it did not materially hinder his freedom of action, and those who saw him frequently ceased, as a rule, to notice it.

His success at Keble, attracting widespread notice, led in the natural course of things to offers of new work.

In 1889 Talbot accepted the important Vicarage of Leeds which he occupied for seven years, gaining direct practical experience of the work of the Church in a great city. He won the affection of all types of men, although there was humorous complaint made by a prominent Leeds citizen: 'You have to be an agnostic or, at least, a Nonconformist before Dr. Talbot takes any interest in you.' But as Dr. Bickersteth, one of his successors at Leeds, has pointed out, 'Alongside of Talbot's instant sympathy with unbelief and keenness to widen his own horizon of truth by occupying another man's standpoint, there went an unfailing pastoral instinct.'

'He's a rum 'un to look at but a good 'un to go,' was the typical verdict of Yorkshiremen concerning him. A different type of man might easily have been ruffled by the Yorkshire temperament but Talbot never felt hurt and whatever was said he always had to examine it, to extract from it what good he could. In my presence, a Yorkshire working man approached him to tell him that his Christianity was all wrong, and I shall never forget the interest which arose in Talbot's face. He sat down forthwith and heard what the man had to say, heedless of its crudeness. He continued to sit listening for some time, and ultimately the two arose in friendship. He had an almost exaggerated capacity for appreciating 'both sides of the question,' so that his family used to chaff him about his love for antinomies— his predilection for 'both . . . and . . .'

Crowds flocked to the Parish Church, not because Talbot was eloquent or popular in his diction, but rather because many found in him one who was manifestly striving to climb the 'Hill Difficulty' of the Christian life, and who, however hesitating his words might sometimes be, yet had a mien and countenance firm and bright in his conviction of the Christian certainties.

He published Sermons Preached in the Parish Church of Leeds 1889–95, but his most notable literary contribution at this time was the little book: Some Titles and Aspects of the Eucharist, the chapters of which were

sermons preached during Eastertide 1894. In their
straightforwardness and simplicity they have been, as
he ventured to hope, of service to many others outside
his own congregation. In the Preface he explains his
purpose:

Among the various ways of considering and representing the
claims of this great Sacrament upon men, I have always felt that
one, not the least convincing or impressive, must be that of tracing
how great lines of human thought and life meet, and focus, and find
their highest expression in it.

To realize this must be a great help to communicants in main-
taining that connection between their Communions and the rest
of life, which is so essential to freshness, consistency, and reality;
it may suggest or deepen trustful and reverent conviction about
Him who in so simple a thing hid such treasures of wisdom, power,
and love. And it may help some who have passed the Sacrament
by as an ecclesiastical ordinance to reconsider entirely its true
meaning and value; and so perhaps to find or find anew Him whom
their souls (sometimes even unconsciously) desire to love.

Possibly there may be a special function for such a way of treating
the Sacrament in the special circumstances of the present and of
the near future. The particular tendency, and I cannot doubt the
particular call, of the time is to a clearer and larger realization of
the corporate and, as it is called, social character of Christian life.
I believe that this has been already accompanied by a fresh realization of divine fitness and meaning in the Sacrament. I am sure
that the Sacrament is what is needed to sanctify, discipline, and
quicken these nobly human and Christian aspirations.

On the translation of Randall Thomas Davidson to
the See of Winchester, Talbot was called to succeed
him as Bishop of Rochester. The diocese included
South London, which, owing to its rapid growth, presented great problems to the Church. He came to his
new work eager and full of zest. The two old houses
in the Kennington Road which had been occupied as
an episcopal residence by Bishop Davidson were super-
seded by Bishop's House, adjacent to Kennington Park.
His family was about him. Gilbert, the joy of the house,
was a small boy. May and Winnie were proud, support-
ing daughters. Edward was approaching ordination,
and Neville was at this time serving in the Rifle Brigade.
The new house was comfortable and commodious.

'ROCHESTER'
Cartoon by 'Spy'

Spy

If the garden was restricted, it was large enough for meetings, and the park was just across the road. Tram-cars and buses ran near by, and on any day the Bishop or Mrs. Talbot or both might be found on them. They trod the common ways and rubbed shoulders with ordinary people, delighted if any one spoke to them.

Talbot's ecclesiastical views were well known. Many who did not see eye to eye with him in matters of importance must have been fearful but in the first few months their fears were largely banished, because it was evident that their new Bishop was a just man, and that it was not the holding of definite views so much as the spirit in which they were held which counted supremely in the making of a Father in God. He made friends with all who came into contact with him. A democrat by conviction, he held that every one in the Church counted, no matter what his position or office.

A writer in the *Manchester Guardian* records a charac-teristic memory of him. It was 'of Dr. Talbot, long after he was made a Bishop, limping up and down the common-room of a certain clergy-house (for he suffered from a stiff knee which made him somewhat lame) and exclaiming: "Yes, yes. The opinion of two such men must have weight. You would know better than I about such matters." The "two such men" were two very junior curates.' Few who met him failed to realize that he would weigh carefully opinions expressed by any one of experience, knowledge, and good will. In this respect he resembled his great predecessor, who, even when Archbishop of Canter-bury, would, when faced with a problem, seek to ascertain the views of any one who chanced to be in his company.

The garden at Kennington proved to be a fitting place for meetings and reunions of all sorts. To it came, as to Keble, many notable men and women of the time who, in the spirit of the house, mixed freely with the guests from near-by parishes, to each and all of whom their Bishop had something to say. He wanted to know about the parishes they came from and the work they did. By such means he cheered and encouraged those whom he regarded as his colleagues in the work of the diocese.

The gatherings usually concluded with a service in the Chapel. Few of his fellow-worshippers will ever forget his absorption and the majesty of his presence as he read with emphasis and power. He read aloud as few men could read, and he loved to do it. He was not always happy as a public speaker, doubting his ability to express himself clearly, but he read aloud with joy and conscious power. In the Chapel his addresses were very simple and untroubled. He felt that he was speaking to a family who were one with him.

He was in the diocese a veritable 'Pastor pastorum.' There was nothing censorious about him. He sought always to cheer and encourage. The parish magazines of the period tell their stories of his beneficent influence, and memories abound still, both of the Bishop and of Mrs. Talbot, who accompanied him whenever possible. Few think of them apart.

On one occasion I walked with him through a Surrey parish. Everything interested him. It was a delightful experience to watch him seeking out people who would talk with him. I was just leaving for Australia, and he charged me with messages to some of his former clergy, particularly to Walter Wragge who had left Woolwich to be Warden at St. Barnabas College at Adelaide, and to Henry Le Fanu, at one time his domestic Chaplain, then Archdeacon of Brisbane, and now Archbishop of Perth. I was proud to carry them and prouder to deliver them.

It was not without trepidation that a young man accepted an invitation to Bishop's House. One never knew whom one might meet, and the Bishop had a habit of leading unexpectedly to the strenuous discussion of social and theological matters, and then, encouraged by his eager and sympathetic attitude, one was betrayed only too easily into youthful dogmatism. However

crude one's remarks might be, one was never allowed
to leave the house before the Bishop had expressed his
gratitude for them.   Talbot's kindly welcome brought
many young men to his luncheon table, where they
found that the mistakes they sometimes made in a
strange environment passed unnoticed in his hospit-
able family circle, and they were tempted in that genial
atmosphere to air their views on matters familiar or
unfamiliar.   One young man, at any rate, remembers
holding forth upon the proper management of a Public
School in the presence of the Bishop's son-in-law,
Lionel Ford, at that time Headmaster of Repton.   It
all seemed so intimate, so easy and delightful.

The Bishop's interest in social matters was intense.
He revealed it to the full later, when in 1918 he presided
over the Archbishops' Committee on Industrial Relations, and inspired a Report which proved to be of
great value and importance.   The problems of Housing
and Employment weighed heavily upon him as they
have done upon his successors in the diocese.   The
Christian Social Union, in which his friends, Henry
Scott Holland and Charles Gore, were specially interested, commanded his ever ready support.   On one
occasion he took the chair at a Christian Social Union
meeting in Holborn Town Hall.   The chief speaker was
Lord Rosebery, whom at that time Londoners flocked
to hear.   The crowd was impatient to hear him, and
the Bishop, failing in his opening speech to take note
of the passage of time, was reminded of this with more
force than politeness.   In a manner and spirit beautiful
beyond all possible expression in words, he accepted the
rebuke.   An electric wave of sympathy flooded the hall
at this manifestation of the finest flower of humility.
The meeting was at once lifted to a higher plane.

His speeches were sometimes confused and prolonged
by his determination to deal fairly with his opponents;
he knew nothing of oratorical invective, he seemed
sometimes to 'wander round' to see if there was any
one or any opinion to which he had been unjust.

Bishop Creighton is reported to have said: 'It is all very fine: but it is quite impossible to be as fair as Talbot talks.' Once, at the Church Assembly, when people were beginning to manifest impatience, Archbishop Davidson rose in great wrath: 'You don't seem to know *who* it is that is speaking to you!'

The unwieldy diocese of Rochester presented a great problem, for it consisted of two distinct parts—South London and the country districts. Directly the division of the diocese was proposed, there was opposition, not only for local reasons. Bishop Talbot faced it manfully. Resistance was mainly inspired by ecclesiastical mistrust coming from those who did not know him. This misunderstanding he overcame, and he fought strenuously and patiently through protracted proceedings in Parliament until the division was accomplished. Then, quite naturally, he turned from the comparative quiet of Rochester to build up the new diocese of Southwark.

He set himself also the task of renovating the historic Church of St. Saviour at Southwark, and made it, both in its structure and in its constitution, a fitting Cathedral Church. As Dean, he took a paternal care in all the details of its adaptation from parochial to diocesan needs. It soon became the spiritual centre of the diocese. In all his work he inspired the ready and enthusiastic help of his colleagues and, whether it was the clergy and Canons of St. Saviour's or the Suffragan Bishops he appointed, they one and all gave him of their best.

In 1911 Talbot felt that he had seen the diocese of Southwark grow to such strength and to so happy a condition that he could leave it without undue regret. His heart was in South London and remained there right to the end, but in that year he accepted the Bishopric of Winchester, and once again was precipitated into the problems of a great diocese.

He delighted greatly in the spacious majesty of Farnham Castle and loved to add to the treasures it contained.

EDWARD STUART TALBOT WHEN BISHOP OF WINCHESTER

Photograph by Bassano

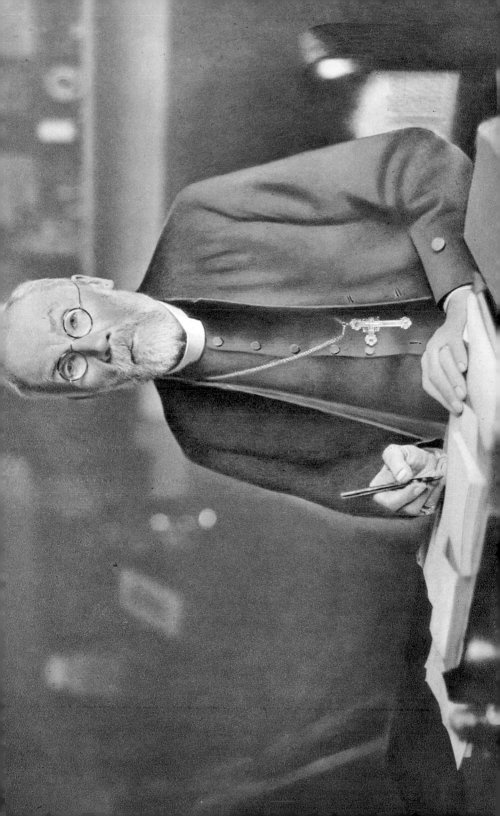

In November 1913, a friend presented an altar cloth. His letter of thanks was characteristic, and reveals much of his nature:

Returning home yesterday I found spread out a beautiful thing of gleaming silk—and waiting till this morning, I found that it took shape as a most beautiful frontal for our Altar; fruit of a promise lightly given, but most faithfully kept. It is immensely admired by those who have seen it. The only drawback is how could any one be sad or tremble in the possession and presence of such a glory? But we must try, perhaps taking it as a symbol of our misused blessings and neglected glories.

But the substitution of blue—my favourite colour and the heavenly one—for sombre black is a shrewd blow at any asceticism. Well, we will take it and use it so that it shall serve the kind giver's purpose of honouring God more, and becoming better people by the touch of His gifts.

I do like connecting my friends with life, by their gifts, and our life with them. So it will often be in thought, remembrance, and prayer, as our eyes rest upon this, in peace, instead of shrinking horrified from its predecessor. But your kindness in thinking of it, and giving it so generously is not to be easily expressed; and, of course, the deepest cause of happiness is the sign that in some way I have been used to help you.

He threw Farnham Castle open as far as he could to the soldiers in the neighbourhood, who wandered there in the enjoyment of its garden, and often he went out to talk to them as friend to friend.

He never avoided an opportunity to take part in conferences or gatherings. One memory comes to mind of a Co-operative Congress at Portsmouth where, after he had spoken, he was followed by a miner who brought a rich gift of humour to play upon the Bishop. Nothing could have afforded greater delight both to the Bishop and to Mrs. Talbot and, though overdue to leave for another engagement, they were unable to tear themselves away. It was all too good to miss. It seldom happens to a Bishop to be humorously 'ragged' in public by a workman.

At Farnham, as elsewhere, he specially loved to be asked to read aloud. On one occasion, to his delight, a visitor asked him to read *The Hound of Heaven*. Mrs.

c

Talbot, the memory of many occasions prompting her, said: 'That will be such a bore. Take care to notice if they are going to sleep.' The Bishop replied: 'I shall not be in the least disturbed if they go to sleep because, if so, I shall know at least they are comfortable.'

'Some of us may remember,' wrote C. G. L. in the *St. Paul's Review*, 'one sunny Sunday afternoon at Farnham Castle when the Bishop, who was always sanguine, gathered into his study his family and the house party to try out an abstruse essay which had been sent him by his friend, Von Hügel. One by one they melted away, but one or two survived even this test.'

On lighter occasions, such as Christmas, when all the children and grandchildren were gathered together, and made more mischievous by the presence of Canon Scott Holland, a Shakespeare play would be read. Each member of the party would adopt a character, except the youngest grandchildren who, being entrusted with the presentation of 'a disturbance without,' construed it with appropriate vigour as the most important feature of the play.

The outbreak of the World War put a severe brake on the development of his plans, and, anxious in his time and place to do all that he could to help humanity in this time of stress, he became absorbed in work which he had not contemplated. It may be said of him that in time of war he strove with all his power to get into the very heart of the Church, and enable it to take an attitude consistent with its mission, not only to Englishmen, but to all men. He was ever ready to serve and to inspire those who, in their several ways, were anxiously praying and working. He became Chairman of a Commission which published *The Army and Religion* as its report.

As indicative of his general attitude, 'An Onlooker' wrote in the *Manchester Guardian*:

I remember well a banquet in Berlin in 1909 at which representatives of the British Churches were fêted—it was the night Bülow was dismissed by the Kaiser—and at which there were very long and rather unreal speeches about peace. Bishop Talbot's turn came and he was on his day. He spoke of the irresistible force of Christian men when acting wholly in dependence on God. 'Against that supernatural power no tyranny can prevail,' he said, as he sat down amid thunderous and spontaneous applause. An English Roman Catholic ecclesiastic turned to me and said: 'Spoken like a true Christian bishop.' Behind Talbot's sometimes hesitating and difficult utterance there burnt an unearthly fire.

The years of war were sad years for him. He felt bitterly being cut off from those in other countries who had been working with him for world friendship through the agency of the Churches. He steadfastly set his face, even after Gilbert's death, against wholesale and undiscriminating condemnation of the whole German people.

When deputations were received at Lambeth he was there at the right hand of the Archbishop, careful not to let any iota of real thought be missed. If a speaker were not understood or had been misinterpreted, it was the Bishop who suggested that he should further explain his position. His help to the Archbishop in those times must have been of incalculable value.

Through it all he did not forget his brethren overseas. The Bishop of North Queensland wrote:

What I want here to record is that we, in North Queensland, owe a special debt of gratitude to the great Bishop Talbot. He was one of the chief leaders of his generation, both spiritually and intellectually. His words at Lambeth Conference carried more weight than those of almost any other man. In the undivided Diocese of Winchester, which included the now separate Dioceses of Portsmouth and Guildford and took in the Channel Islands, he had one of the most exacting tasks in the whole Anglican Communion, but he found time to help North Queensland as a Vice-President of our auxiliary, and he took a deep interest in all that we did. When I was in England he wanted to be told all that was going on here, and it was a great delight to tell him. Through the greatness of his mind and heart he had time for every one who needed his help, sympathy, or wise advice. And there was no more perfect hospitality in the world than that of Farnham Castle.

At the end of his episcopate the vast diocese was divided into three. As the projects and plans for the division of the diocese developed, he was anxious and much perplexed as to the place of the Bishop's residence. He himself loved Farnham, and could not with equanimity contemplate leaving it, difficult as it must have been for him to maintain. For him the question was ultimately settled by his resignation in 1923.

It was a severe wrench to him to give up his office as Bishop of Winchester and he felt, perhaps, as other men in high position have felt, that once he left he would become unwanted. But there were, in fact, far too many who wanted to enjoy his presence and listen to him. A fellow Bishop describes the grace of his retirement: 'venturesome, cheerful, clear and strong, a daily wonder.'

It was a great delight to him to attend special services in connection with the institutions he loved, not desiring to be the chief figure, but just to participate in the acts of worship. As founder of Lady Margaret Hall he laid the foundation stone of its beautiful chapel, and on January 14th, 1933, he dedicated the completed building. In spite of increasing deafness and a recent accident resulting in a broken thigh, he rose to the great occasion in all his 'magnificence.' 'Those who were present,' wrote a correspondent in *The Times*, 'will not easily forget the sound of Dr. Talbot's voice ringing through the beautiful buildings. Few institutions can have had a founder who laid its foundations more wisely and securely, or whose life was a more perfect example to its members.' He acted as though he were back in the Keble days. He visited Oxford friends, talking and listening as a young man facing new tasks.

Later in the year 1933, delighted to revisit his old diocese, he dedicated a small room which had been set apart as a chapel for the members of the Student Christian Movement in the Rachel McMillan Training College. The little room, to him at least, was sacred as a great cathedral. He had made himself acquainted with every detail of the life of Margaret McMillan, and in a prophetic way he dealt with her life's work.

To the students present he gave the feeling that they were his friends and they will long remember him. As always, he was accompanied by Mrs. Talbot, who, also in spite of advancing years, was keenly alive to all that passed. On his departure he asked hesitatingly whether they would like his photograph. To his great happiness his offer was accepted, and the picture hangs with a suitable inscription in the chapel.

At times he was a real anxiety to his friends because of his enterprise. Lame as he was, he was ready for any adventure. On one occasion he slipped badly and broke his thigh. There were long weeks of inaction at 45 Lexham Gardens, but his convalescence gave him an opportunity to receive his friends. He enjoyed his books, both serious and light. A visitor found him, on one occasion, revelling in a novel by P. G. Wodehouse brought him by the Bishop of London. Although he was obviously suffering, his mind was still active, and, as in the old days, the hour's talk allowed was strenuous in the extreme.

He once paid a visit to Welwyn Garden City. He had just been suffering from eye trouble and, delighting in his recovered sight, he had provided himself with a map, and in the car on the way down every outstanding place, whether lane or gate or country house or main road, had to be identified. His eager interest was that of a child taken out for the first time. As an example of the working of true education he stood supreme, in that he preserved all the fine qualities of a child in spite of his eighty-six years. He had seen the beginning of Letchworth Garden City and had taken an active interest in it, speaking about it and advocating it at various meetings, including an annual meeting of the Co-operative Permanent Building Society, but Welwyn Garden City was new to him and he was keen to see it. In this 'City' there are no objects of historical interest, but he insisted on visiting the central squares, the temporary church, and everything there was. He was delighted at its proximity to Hatfield House, which had been in many senses a home to him all his life.

Bishop Talbot's last years were especially happy because of the work of his sons and daughters, and the delightful promise of his grandchildren. He missed greatly his son Neville, labouring as Bishop of Pretoria, but was cheered by frequent records of his work and an occasional book. Ultimately he had the joy of welcoming Neville home when he became Vicar of St. Mary's, Nottingham.

It was a sight to see the Bishop at Lord's, when his grandson, Neville Ford, was playing in the Varsity match. He had always loved cricket and to watch people at play.

The death of Gilbert, his youngest son, in the war was an abiding sorrow. Gilbert was so brilliant, and so promising, and he had looked forward to this son's taking his part in the world of statesmanship. The foundation of Toc H, with Gilbert's memory as an inspiration, shot his sorrow through with great happiness.

With great pride he heard his son Edward preach at Oxford on the occasion of the Centenary of the Tractarian Movement which had inspired him in the days of his youth, and to which he had always adhered in faithful gratitude.

On January 25th, 1934, he attended the requiem for his lifelong friend Lord Halifax at St. Mary's, Graham Street. During the evening of the same day, for the last time in his life, he worshipped in public at a service held in Southwark Cathedral for Church people of the diocese: 'A Pilgrimage of Praise and Thanksgiving for the Goodness of God in inspiring the prayer and work and sacrifice of those who raised the Twenty-Five Churches Fund.' To him it was joy unspeakable. He stood, as many noted at the time, taking full part, proud to be in the company of the clergy and laity of his old diocese, side by side with two of his successors in the Bishopric, Cyril Garbett, who also succeeded him at Winchester, and Richard Parsons, still in the opening years of his episcopate. It would be difficult to do justice to the happiness with which the older among the laity welcomed him among them. One old man proudly told me, his face lighting up, that the Bishop in leaving had inadvertently placed his stick heavily upon his foot, and had asked his pardon. He would never forget it. The incident was insignificant, but it was symbolical of the intense veneration and affection of many in South London for the great man who had moved among them as Bishop twenty-three years before.

The next day he went to the circus at Olympia. He watched the performance, as joyous and wondering as any one of the children among whom he sat.

In the evening of January 30th he passed from this life 'swiftly and gently' as a child falls to sleep.

He was a gallant gentleman, a noble Bishop, a faithful Father in God. The Archbishop of Canterbury, at the Funeral Service, spoke to all his friends present and absent:

'At this service of praise and thanksgiving, I bid you give thanks to God for the life and the example and the memory of Edward Stuart Talbot. Let us give thanks for the gifts and counsel and strength with which he guided and encouraged God's Church and people as a faithful and wise steward, bringing forth from his treasures, both old and new, the old abiding truth of the Catholic Faith, enriched and enlightened by new thought and knowledge. . . . In the name of the Church to which he gave his loyalty and service during a lifetime of wellnigh ninety years we bid farewell in love and gratitude to this noble-minded and great-hearted Father in God.'

CHARLES GORE
1853–1932

Fellow of Trinity College, Oxford	1875–95
Hon. Fellow ,, ,,	1895–1919
Vice-Principal of Cuddesdon .	1880–3
Principal of the Pusey House .	1884–93
Vicar of Radley . . .	1893–4
Canon of Westminster . .	1894–1902
Bishop of Worcester. . .	1902–5
Bishop of Birmingham . .	1905–11
Bishop of Oxford . . .	1911–19
On staff of King's College, London	1919–32

In hoc signo vinces is the motto of all the Gores. It was the battle cry of Charles Gore, 'who, by his life and teaching, was wont to lead all to higher things.' [1]

It is not difficult to estimate the place of Charles Gore in the life of his time. There is in that respect a natural unanimity of witness.

Oxford affectionately mourns Charles Gore as one of the most illustrious as well as the most loyal of her sons. A thinker, a preacher, a social reformer, a vigorous administrator of three dioceses, and a saint, he has left an imperishable mark on the development of the Church and religion of his country.[2]

Charles Gore came of a family aristocratic in tradition and temper, Whig in politics, and sound Church in religion. From its admixture of English and Irish ancestry it inherited the seriousness of the former and the lightheartedness of the latter. The Gores had their roots in London. They were city magnates in the sixteenth century, but, having passed to Ireland, the head of the house was created Earl of Arran in 1762, with his seat at Castle Gore, Co. Mayo.

[1] Latin Oration. Senior Proctor, University of Oxford.
[2] Review of Year 1932. Vice-Chancellor, University of Oxford.

Charles Alexander Gore, father of the Bishop and a younger brother of the fourth Earl, came to London after service as a page in the Vice-Regal Court at Dublin, to seek a career in the Public Service, becoming ultimately Commissioner of Woods and Forests. In 1845 he married Augusta, daughter of the Earl of Bessborough, and widow of the Earl of Kerry. Of this happy marriage five children, Francis, Spencer, Emily, Charles, and Caroline were born. The family was an expression of English life at its best, united in days of sorrow as in days of happiness. Charles, as a third son, was naturally of no special importance, the more so since Francis [1] and Spencer,[2] his elder brothers, were remarkably gifted. The former became a distinguished lawyer, Recorder of Canterbury, and Solicitor to the Board of Inland Revenue, and the latter was a prominent athlete, representing England at both cricket and lawn tennis.

Charles rarely talked of his early days either in private or in public. He joined in the games and activities of his brothers and their friends, among them Henry Scott Holland, who lived near by at Wimbledon. Yet in boyhood as through life, in spite of many friendships and an intense love of his kind, he was in reality a lonely spirit. His sister Emily mothered him, as her diary reveals. In his seventh year he caught a glimpse of the big world, going with his brothers and sisters to a children's fancy-dress ball at Buckingham Palace. It was probably in preparation for this that he became an unwilling pupil at a dancing class. With the rest of the family he attended, as he tells us, 'very Low Church services.'

In 1862, at the age of nine, he followed his brothers to May Place, Malvern, famous then as an upper-class preparatory school.

It must have been immediately prior to, or just after, his entry to May Place that (to quote almost the only

---

[1] Sir Francis Gore, K.C.B. Born 1846, still living.
[2] Spencer William Gore. Born 1850, died 1906.

autobiographical excursion which he allowed himself in his writing) :

I read a book by a Protestant author—a Presbyterian, I think— entitled *Father Clement,* about the conversion of a Catholic priest to Protestantism. I have never read it since. I had been brought up in ordinary old-fashioned English Church ways. I had attended only very Low Church services. I had never heard of the Oxford Movement. I knew nothing about Catholicism, except as a strange superstition called Popery. But the book described confession and absolution, fasting, the Real Presence, the devotion of the Three Hours, the use of incense, etc., and I felt instinctively and at once that this sort of sacramental religion was the religion for me.[1]

He entered Harrow in 1866, the *Annus Mirabilis* of Henry Montagu Butler. To Butler himself Gore owed much, and described him as 'an immense force for righteousness.' The School was Whig and Evangelical. Spencer Gore was its athletic idol, and Charles was very much 'Young Gore,' although as his scholarship developed he gained a place of his own. 'I remember once,' writes Lord Desborough, 'seeing his father walking down the High Street at Harrow on Speech Day between his two sons and I looked on him with great interest as the father of two of the foremost boys in the School, the one in athletics and the other in scholarship, and the old man looked very proud.' For one reason, at least, 'young Gore' was popular. If put on to construe, he would go on translating, says C. J. Longman, 'to the limits of the prescribed lesson and beyond.' This is thought to have inspired the school song:

> Where has he got to?
> Tell him not to!
> This is the lesson for next July.

His great friend was Marsham Argles.[2] They were known as 'inseparables,' and became the centre of a little group of 'devout, keen, catholic-minded Christians,' pious, but not priggish.

It was at Harrow that he consciously determined to

[1] *Belief in God,* 1921. Preface, page xi.
[2] Argles accompanied Gore to Balliol, became Principal of St. Stephen's House and died in 1888 in the service of the Oxford Mission to Calcutta.

CHARLES GORE

Painted by John Mansbridge for King's College in the University of London.

live, as nearly as it was possible for a man to do, on the lines, both in general and in detail, of the life of Jesus in the world. A sermon on 'The Disciplined Life,' preached by Brooke Foss Westcott, affected him profoundly. It may well be that it planted in his mind the germinal idea of the Community of the Resurrection.

'We want a rule,' said the preacher, 'which shall answer to the complexity of our own age. We want a discipline which shall combine the sovereignty of soul of Antony, the social devotion of Benedict, the humble love of Francis, the matchless energy of the Jesuits with faith that fears no trial, with hope that fears no darkness, with truth that fears no light.

'I cannot but pray every one who hears me to listen humbly to the promptings of God's spirit, if so be that he is even now calling him to take a foremost part in it.'

Seldom has there been such a preacher, seldom such a listener. After Gore's death the *Harrovian* linked them together. 'If saintliness and surpassing intellect are looked upon as the chief elements of greatness, Bishop Gore may stand first on our roll of honour, though on such reasoning Bishop Westcott would be his chief rival.'

The Gore who left Harrow in July 1871 was in all fundamentals the same Gore who laboured persistently until his death on January 17th 1932. 'I come by my faith as Christians have always come by it,' he wrote in a letter to Sir Oliver Lodge on December 1st 1907, 'by receiving the word of God and then (so far as it has been erroneously understood) seeking to correct it or verify it, both in life and speculation.'

He won a scholarship at Balliol and entered Oxford, firmly rooted in the faith. This being so it was all to the good that he became a scholar of a College which was, in the best sense of the word, 'secular.' Even though he was not a typical Balliol man of his time, he made contact with many notable minds.

Benjamin Jowett had been Master of the College for some twelve months before Gore entered it. He has been called an 'orthodox heretic.' Balliol was his passion, and he was determined to attract to it by means of scholarships the best men, whether from the streets, the Public Schools, or from other colleges. He desired to unite more closely the different classes of society, to promote more friendly relations between different denominations, and to combine the teaching both of theology and science into one coherent system of thought. His attitude of detached reverence was good for a young man of Gore's type with its tendency, at least, to becoming narrow.

Thomas Hill Green was at that time Tutor in Philosophy. Gore, like most Balliol men, loved and honoured him. He absorbed much of his teaching and outlook, gaining thereby, in common with such a man as Arnold Toynbee, purity of social purpose and a new dynamic. Green's anti-ecclesiastical bias, however, did not affect him in the least.

At Oxford, as always, Gore loved argument and intellectual skirmishes. 'It was a regular joke at Balliol,' said Argles to his sister, 'that whenever anyone expressed an opinion, Gore used to say, with an agonized look: "Oh, I don't agree with you."'

In general he was remote from the College life. There are few of his contemporaries living to bear witness, but among them is Sir Richard Lodge, who writes:

He, doubtless, had his own friends, but he was not in close touch with what was in my eyes the dominant set in the College. This set, which included men like Thomas Raleigh and Herbert Warren, centred round H. H. Asquith, who, in my first term, was elected to a Fellowship, and resided in College during his probationary year before going on to the Bar. The tone of this set, and of the College as a whole, was unquestionably secular. Gore, on the other hand, occupied, even in these early years, a sort of ecclesiastical primacy which was not all together acceptable to his juniors. For example, there was an understanding that on those Sundays when the Chapel was filled to hear the Master preach, Gore had a right to read the lessons. With youthful presumption I determined, not without encouragement from my contemporaries, to defy this unwritten convention. It was my week in rotation to read the lessons, and I made an early start for the lectern. Gore also started, but had to return to his seat on discovering that he had been forestalled. At the moment I exulted, but I subsequently repented. Not long afterwards an undergraduate died in college. Such an event always makes a great impression in a small community, but what impressed me most was the discovery that Gore had sat up for more than one night with the dying youth. This opened my eyes to the real spiritual eminence of the Senior Scholar, whose elocution I had been so ready to challenge. From that time I realized that the College harboured an unappreciated saint. In later years, I had occasional glimpses of Gore. And I never lost the sense of his spiritual ascendancy which I had been forced, almost against my will, to admit during our undergraduate days.

In 1875 he was elected a Fellow of Trinity College. This gave him much happiness at the time and throughout his life. His triumphant telegram to his mother has been preserved:

C. Gore,   To the Countess of Kerry,
   Bulliol,   Surrey,
      Oxford.   June 15 1875.

    I have been elected Fellow of Trinity will come home on Thursday.

The days of initial preparation over, he grew apace in knowledge, wisdom, and power. In due time he was ordained, and served successively during vacations and week-ends in two Liverpool parishes, Christ Church, Bootle, and St. Margaret's, Princes Road, Liverpool. If it had not been for his definite views on 'Evening Communion,' he could have become Vicar of one of them. His personality was already an inspiration and a revelation.

In 1880 be became Vice-Principal of Cuddesdon under Charles Wellington Furse, often travelling all night from Liverpool in order that he might lecture on the Monday morning. He delighted in the work of the College. His Principal, prophesying the greatness of the service he was destined to render to the cause of truth, said: 'Whatever he says or does he bears witness to the reality of the Presence of God.'

It was his habit, persisted in until his death, to walk every afternoon. At Cuddesdon he could always find a companion, fit and willing, to take long tramps, footpaths or no footpaths, in the valley of the Thame.

'As a child I loved him,' writes Bishop Furse, 'as I believe all children did.' His humour found free and acceptable flow. He, as Vice-Principal, in common parlance 'The Vice,' was reading during silence at dinner from the *Imitation*, when coming to the sentence, 'One vice must be extirpated every year,' he burst out laughing, 'which,' says my informant, 'was most contagious.' He related how he grew his beard. 'I did it when staying at a big country-house in Ireland where there was a large party of smart young people. It was very hard to do; and I had to meditate a great deal on the four last things before I was able to get through with it.'

Marsham Argles, probably the closest friend Gore ever had, was Principal of St. Stephen's House in Calcutta, and this led Gore to pay his first visit to India. At heart he was a missionary, longing to hasten the day when 'all nations should bring glory and honour to the City of God.' He was one of the founders of the Oxford Mission to Calcutta, and all through his life he took a keen and active interest in it. Even in his last year he visited it.

On his return from his first visit, largely by the influence of Liddon, who saw in him one supremely equipped to interpret the ideals and churchmanship of Edward Bouverie Pusey, he was appointed to be Principal Librarian of the newly-founded Pusey House, with Vincent Stuckey Coles and Frank Brightman as colleagues. A well-known Oxford Divine was asked how the three Librarians would occupy themselves. 'Oh, Brightman will talk about the books, and Coles will dust them, but Gore will read them.'

Dr. Hollis, Bishop of Taunton, gives us a glimpse of him as he was in this office:

One of my most cherished memories is of Sunday evenings when he had been out somewhere preaching. He could not go to sleep easily after this. So he used to come to my room, and the conversation always began with the same three words : 'Got any baccy? (He never seemed to have any.) Bring some down and I 'll read to you.' I went down and he produced an old pipe tied with string and sealing-wax. The reading always began with poetry, generally short poems, and each reminded him of another, until the floor round his chair was littered with books. Burke's speeches sometimes took turns with the poets. Then he would leave the books and begin telling stories about people, which he could do admirably and most amusingly. He had the keenest sense of humour and was always full of fun. On these occasions I was invariably alone with him, and he just gave himself up to the relaxation which was necessary to him after the strain of preaching. It was sheer delight to have him like that. (He was so many-sided, and always ready to enter into any news which you might bring to him.)

The evening often ended characteristically. As he told story after story he would first wriggle up into his arm-chair, and then gradually wriggle out of it on to the hearth-rug. Perhaps that is not the picture which most people have of the famous Principal of Pusey House, but it is Charles Gore in one of his most delightful moods.

Characteristically, whenever Gore was overburdened or in need of rest, he turned, as it seemed light-heartedly, to the humorous aspects of life. At such times he loved to make fun and to be made fun of. After one story, at which all laughed, he said that, the last time he told it, a clergyman said : 'Oh, dear, I 've not laughed so much since my dear wife died! '

The Pusey House days were set in serious times, and Gore was in deadly earnest. He worked in season and out of season, enduring the disappointments which ever accompany adventurous leadership.

'The first Principal (Charles Gore) who was the virtual founder of the Pusey House, left behind him the memory of three great movements — the Reconciliation of Catholicism and Modern Thought, the Consecration by Faith of Social Work, and the expansion of the idea of the Religious Life in England.'[1] These movements are symbolized by *Lux Mundi*, published in 1889, and the Bampton Lectures on *The Incarnation of the Son of God*, delivered during Lent 1891 ; the foundation of

[1] *Life of V. S. S. Coles* (second Principal) by J. F. Briscoe.

the Christian Social Union in 1880; and the creation of the Community of the Resurrection in 1887.

In Oxford itself Gore exercised great influence on the prevalent thought of the University. It is difficult for us at this time to realize how powerful he was, but his contemporaries were unanimous concerning him, both those who approved his views and those who sought to controvert them. Canon George Borlase writes:

Many of us undergraduates were very sceptical about the fundamental truths of religion, and at times inclined to regard Christianity as an outworn superstition. But we had the feeling that if a man so morally and intellectually supreme as Gore could believe and dedicate all he had and was to the cause of Christ, then, at any rate, the Christian Faith was something that we could not lightly dismiss.

The outstanding fact for many of us was that one who was prepared to take on the champions of reason upon their own ground should have been able to maintain the traditional position of the Christian Faith.

In 1889 he lectured in Trinity College on the Incarnation to such a large audience that the place had to be changed from the Lecture Room to the Hall.

A course of Sunday evening sermons which he preached at All Saints, Oxford, about this time are worthy to be remembered together with the Bamptons and the great time at the Abbey. The present Dean of York describes them as 'a sort of rehearsal for Westminster,' and continues:

I think that what fascinated us in them was not merely their moral overwhelmingness, but that sense which Gore then conveyed to his hearers that he was wrestling through his subject with them, letting the argument bear him whither it would, living through his own discourse as an adventure and an experience. And, incidentally, it was in those sermons (as far as one could tell) that he first hammered out a whole series of paragraphs—or pages —which became a permanent part of his preaching outfit, and would through all his life recur again and again, and were the joy, sometimes the slightly amused delight, of those who loved him—as Coleridge says of the fixed stars, in the margin of the *Ancient Mariner*, 'and yet there is a silent joy at their arrival.'

In this year *Lux Mundi* was published. It had been

planned in 1887 at a meeting of 'the Holy Party'—
a group of friends which included Gore, Talbot, Illingworth, Scott Holland, Francis Paget, and others.
Later, at a meeting held in Scott Holland's house in
Amen Court, St. Paul's, it was found that no chapter
had been written on the Holy Spirit, and Gore was asked
to write it. The result was the celebrated chapter which
aroused tremendous opposition at the time, but which
opened the way for the Catholic party in the Church
to accept freely the best results of modern scientific
thought.

Bishop Nash, who was at that time a resident in the
Pusey House, has summed up the position:

In the autumn of 1889 *Lux Mundi* appeared and at once one
essay was singled out for reprobation. This was Gore's Essay on
the Holy Spirit, in which he frankly accepted much of the advanced
textual and literary criticism of the Old Testament. It was a bold
departure and even very good men were startled.

The value of so much else in *Lux Mundi* did not for the time
gain due appreciation. As has happened with Lambeth and other
pronouncements it might have seemed that it dealt with no matter
but Old Testament criticism.

Gore did not falter, but he suffered intensely at this time. He
had, perhaps, hardly foreseen the bitterness of the opposition.
Himself utterly solid in adherence to the Creed, he had learned
how much of doubt and unbelief was caused by wrong views on
the inspiration of Scripture, and he was sure the question must be
faced. He felt that he was being misunderstood, and that time
would bring calmer judgment; but he was sorely grieved, and
especially at the pain and distress he had caused to Dr. Liddon.

Gore wrote to Liddon from the Pusey House on
October 25th 1889:

I hear from Paget that evil rumours have reached you of our
essay book, *Lux Mundi*. I believe you will approve almost all of it.
What you will least like are a few pages at the end, I am afraid,
of my essay. I send it herewith, so that, if you wish, you may
know the worst. Only I hope if you read it you will read the
whole essay. . . . Whatever I have said there I have said times
out of number to people of all classes in difficulties, and they found,
again and again, that it helped them to a firm footing in Catholic
Faith. Where you have found a certain method spiritually effective
and useful, and you believe it to be quite orthodox, it seems

impossible to refrain from saying it. Something had to be said on the subject. I do sincerely hope that, if you read it, you will not seriously disapprove. I think I should almost die of it if it did harm. But certainly experience has led me to hope otherwise. If you seriously disapprove, it would be a great misery. But at least I had better send it without delay.

To Liddon, the essay caused the utmost pain and dismay. He wrote to Lord Halifax on February 19th 1890:

I knew and loved his general character. I knew that he was sound about the Incarnation and the Sacraments, and I did not suspect that he had constructed a private kennel for liberalizing ideas in Theology within the precincts of the Old Testament, and as much of the New Testament as bears upon it.

When Dr. Liddon was dying, Gore was one of the few friends he desired to see, but it can hardly be doubted that, in spite of this reconciliation in the spirit, Liddon's condemnation of his *Lux Mundi* essay had a marked effect upon Gore's thought, tending to check his advance along lines of thought which were later travelled by some of his younger contemporaries.

Public prominence was given to the whole matter largely by the bitter attacks made by Father Ignatius, who engaged the Town Hall at Oxford and placarded the city. Bishop Hollis describes Gore's attitude to Ignatius's attacks: 'I was living at Pusey House at that time as a layman. Gore sent me to the Town Hall to hear what was said. On my return he came to my room and I gave him a full report. He remarked only, "Funny old thing," and returned to his work.'

The attacks culminated in a dramatic protest made by Father Ignatius at the Birmingham Church Congress in 1893. An account, written by C. M. Hudson, reveals much that was characteristic of Gore:

When Canon Gore (as he then was) came on to the platform and opened his lips to read, there was a slight commotion as Father Ignatius rose up starkly and strode forward. I heard later that he pulled out his crucifix and cursed the reader. Fanaticism was in every lineament—the other wore the face of a man who prayed. The subject of Gore's paper was reunion with Nonconformists, and he took the line that no organic union was (then) possible. Before he could finish, the chairman's bell rang, and he stopped as though he had been shot. A later speaker gave us the unforgettable last words he had not had time to utter. They were to the effect that, though corporate reunion was not possible, we could all cultivate personal religious friendships with Nonconformists. I learnt subsequently that during the Congress week he had been the guest of the great Congregationalist minister, Dr. Dale of Birmingham.

Gore had many friends among Nonconformists, yet throughout his life he fought any attempt to depart from the creeds and rubrics of the Church of England. He would have no watering down of the Creeds. The Church to him at its altars and in its pulpits was the holy place of those alone who *ex animo* accepted its Faith. To some he seemed narrow, yet he saw the whole of humanity as illumined by the 'logos light.' He was eager that the Church should recognize and welcome truth coming from any source whatsoever and consecrate it in the service of God and man. There is a glorious passage in the *Mission of the Church* which reveals the splendour of his vision:

Already in the history of Christianity it has appeared how each fresh race, as it has been brought within the Church, has both itself found its sanctification there, and also has brought out some fresh aspect of the full meaning of Christ. It was but a very small part of Christianity which emerged in the purely Jewish Church. The Greek race, with its unique powers of intellect, had for its vocation to bring out the treasures of wisdom which lay hid in Christ. To it, in the main, we owe our theology. The Roman race, with its wonderful powers of discipline and organization, built up the medieval papacy, that glorious witness to the governing and disciplining forces of Christianity. The Teutonic race has surely taught the world much that it would not otherwise have known of the power of Christianity in consecrating individual character. And there still remain great and rich gifts for consecration; the subtilty of the Hindus, the patience of the Chinese, the geniality and gentleness of the Japanese. Here are great qualities not yet, except in small measure, sanctified in Christ; and we shall not see the full glory of Christianity till these alien races are brought inside the circle of the Church, to bring unsuspected treasures of wisdom and beauties of character out of the same old and unchanging creed.

Brethren, in the Apocalypse there is set before us the picture of the perfected Church. It is completely catholic—'a great multitude which no man could number of all nations and kindreds and people and tongues'; it is absolutely one—'the city that lieth four-square,' and from within its walls goes up the harmony of perfected praise. Again, it is wholly pure: the Bride of Christ, in white raiment, the perfected righteousness of the saints. Lastly, it is triumphant and acknowledged of all as 'the kings of the earth bring their glory and honour into it.' Catholic, one, pure, triumphant—we shall behold her, but not now; we shall see her, but not nigh. It is the vision of heaven but it is the hope of earth.

After a second visit to India in 1890 Gore delivered the famous Bampton Lectures on *The Incarnation of the Son of God*. The University Church was packed on each occasion. Many perchance hoped to hear new things, or even heresy, advanced by the editor of *Lux Mundi*. What they heard was 'the outpouring by a loyal and devoted Anglican of a burning personal faith in Jesus Christ, God and Man,' concluding with a noble appeal to the young men who were his hearers:

To you, then, brethren, to you more particularly before whom life yet lies in opening promise, the document of God's offer in Jesus Christ is once again presented. It is black with the signatures, it is red with the seals, of those who, in the generations that are passed or passing away, have given in their assent 'that God is true,' and have handed on to you the results of their faithful witness. You cannot evade your responsibilities; you must at the last issue confess or deny; you must sign or repudiate. Summon, then, to your aid every heavenly power to assist you in the great surrender which they make who, having steadily in view all that is involved in faith in Jesus Christ, 'set to their seals' for time and for eternity 'that God is true.'

It was the appeal of his life. He repeated it twenty-four years later at the end of his Mission to Undergraduates at Oxford in Lent 1914.

In these lectures Gore stood, as it were, on a mountain of transfiguration. It was the high time in his life. Ever after it would seem the vision he then saw so clearly sufficed him. He had seen the Lord and was satisfied, and for the rest of his life he was content to reaffirm and expound the truth as he saw it, and to translate into the common life with all his power the divine reality. Henceforth, he stood before men as prophet, expositor, and Bishop, a warrior of the Cross, but he had made his supreme adventure. Thus it was that, when later theologians travelled further on a way he had opened up, he never travelled with them. He watched them anxiously, and if they deviated from the path as he saw it then he pronounced warnings, often in sorrow.

While at the Pusey House, Gore founded the Community of the Resurrection. It was to work in the world. At first it was a provisional brotherhood striving to create an appropriate rule. On July 25th 1892, the first six made profession, for thirteen months, of poverty, celibacy, and obedience. Gore was elected Senior, not caring to be called Superior. There was no life vow. He remained in the Community until he was consecrated Bishop.

In September 1893 he accepted the Vicarage of Radley, near Oxford, and moved there, accompanied by early members of the Community of the Resurrection. Although, owing to ill-health, he only spent a few months in the village, yet the memories of him are still vivid.

A parishioner tells us:

The Three Hours Service on Good Friday 1894 is still a memory. Such a small congregation, and indifferent music. A few village people coming and going, a few members of Radley College with their visitors. Thousands must have heard Charles Gore give these addresses in great churches and cathedrals in later years. Was he ever more intense or more practical than he was at Radley that day? He had already known much suffering himself, hence his words went home with poignancy to the hearts of his hearers. 'There are times of difficulty when religion seems barren and dry. There is a depth in human nature below these, in which we may swear that, be it with pleasure or without it, be it with satisfaction or not, be it with joy or gloom, I will hear, I will obey.' Was this occasion also the first on which in these addresses he quoted the lines from Frederic Myers's *St. Paul*:

'Desperate tides of the whole great world's anguish
Forced thro' the channels of a single heart.'

In August 1894 he was ordered to rest until

November, but he had no sooner recovered than he was called to be a Canon of Westminster and was installed in January 1895.

His advent to the Abbey pulpit proved to be an outstanding event. He drew multitudes to listen to him and to worship with him. One of the clergy serving with him at that time writes:

The attraction of his Lectures on Fridays in Lent after Evensong and his sermons when in residence was wonderful. 'Nothing like it since Charles Kingsley,' was remarked by one of the Abbey Canons. People found their way into the organ loft when the Choir and Transepts were full. It was a wonderful sight, and to this day many feel that it would have been well if he had remained in Westminster.

Some of the members of the Community moved with him from Radley to 4 Little Cloisters, his Abbey lodgings. His house became a centre for many who gathered for discussion of living problems in Church and State. His welcome was warm. It was given to every one. He delighted particularly then, as always, to encourage and help young men facing their work in life. Their difficulties were his difficulties and their successes his also.

For myself, meeting Gore in those early days was entry into a new and wider life. Looking back over the years, I see myself again as a youth of eighteen years, who had moved only in narrow ways and had never met any one of more than local importance, being admitted at once, without question, to friendship with him and to the fellowship of the members of the Community, Walter Frere, John Nash, Paul Bull, and Richard Rackham among them. In Gore's study there were long and unhurried talks. Then at supper and after, there was conversation in which Gore, thinking aloud, always took a part. For his young guest, encouraged to put his thoughts into words, it was a liberal education.

Oxford saw the days of Gore's adventurous thought; Westminster saw the equally great days of his expository genius and prophetic fire. His expositions of the Sermon on the Mount, Ephesians and Romans were delivered as lectures. They struck a new note in sacred literature. They swelled in many a heart to songs of high endeavour. At times he would start to preach haltingly and uneasily. Then it would seem that he was caught up in the spirit and no words can express the flame of his power.

After preaching, just as in Pusey House days, he became intensely human and full of quiet fun, greatly enjoying a pipe. 'I can sit still and smoke, but I can't sit still and do nothing.'

The days at Westminster were all too few. In December 1901 he accepted the offer of the Bishopric of Worcester.

Dr. Henson, at that time a fellow Canon, preaching in the Abbey pulpit, said:

The loss of Westminster is the gain of the whole Church. . . . Thank God, that the great population of the Midlands will hence-forth see in the principal seat of spiritual authority one who commends his messages by fearless honesty, apostolic zeal and personal sanctity. I believe, nay I confidently expect that, if God in mercy to his Church grant strength and years, the Episcopate which is about to begin in the diocese of Worcester will take rank in our ecclesiastical records as in a rare degree illustrious and fruitful.

The expectation was abundantly fulfilled.

His way to the Bishopric was made singularly difficult by the action of the Church Association and the National Protestant League in presenting a Petition of Right to the King against the appointment. When the appointed day for the consecration arrived, the matter was still not legally concluded, though there could be no doubt of the outcome. The Provost of Southwell, at the time Chaplain to the Archbishop of Canterbury, has described his visit to Gore's house on the day before that fixed for the consecration. 'Gore wrote to Archbishop Temple saying he could not be consecrated till the legal matter was settled. Temple told him that Kensit was wrong and that he must be consecrated as arranged. Gore still refused. On the evening before the day fixed, Temple sent me over to ask Gore once again what he would do. Never can I forget the scene in his study. Gore sat on the hearthrug, tied himself into a knot of agony, wrestling with the problem of obedience, and at last said "No."

'Next morning seventeen Bishops met in Jerusalem Chamber and Moberly, too, was there to preach the sermon. But Gore was not there.
So Temple said he would pro-
ceed to consecrate Trower as
Bishop of Likoma and preach
the sermon himself. This he did
at the last minute on "Foreign
Missions."' [1]

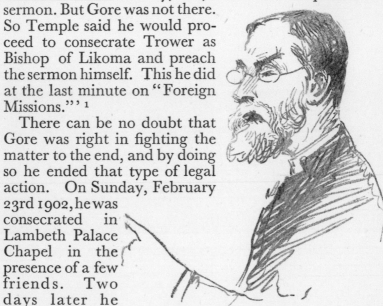

There can be no doubt that
Gore was right in fighting the
matter to the end, and by doing
so he ended that type of legal
action. On Sunday, February
23rd 1902, he was
consecrated in
Lambeth Palace
Chapel in the
presence of a few
friends. Two
days later he
was enthroned
in Worcester Ca-
thedral as the

CHARLES GORE WHEN BISHOP OF WORCESTER
From a pencil sketch by the Dean of Westminster

104th Bishop. 'I pray from my very heart that I may not too grievously disappoint the hopes of my friends.'

At Worcester he set new standards for the episcopal office, as he had done for the Canons of West-minster. 'He undoubtedly added something of great significance to our conception of what a modern Bishop ought to do and be.' [2] It has been said of him that he shrank from the office of Bishop. In a deep and sacred sense it is true, but it gave him joy to be called

[1] From an article in the *Church of England Newspaper*, January 29th 1932.
[2] Canon Peter Green, in the *Manchester Guardian*.

CHARLES GORE

*A drawing by John Mansbridge now in the National
Portrait Gallery*

Charles Gore

to the highest order in the Church. He dedicated all his energies meticulously to fulfil overwhelming duties. Gore was thorough in all that he did. Nothing was too small for his attention and he could not delegate. His Chaplains, first the Rev. J. Reader Smith and then the Rev. Wilfred Cooper, were ideal but they could only assist, not lessen, his multifarious activities.

There were many who deplored his withdrawal from his supreme task as scholar and expositor. In a sense they were right, for it is clear that, in spite of notable sermons and utterances, he never regained the highest level of his previous work. Even of the last ten years of freedom this is true, despite the excellence of his Trilogy, *The Reconstruction of Belief*, and his notable Gifford Lectures, *The Philosophy of the Good Life*.

Certain Churchmen, who differed from him in matters of ritual or in sacramental doctrine, feared his appointment; but they little knew him. He was just and fair. Under his rule all men who were faithful to the central doctrines of the Church had their chance. Slackness he abhorred. Although of aristocratic temper, he was full of humility. Men might differ from him but he was ever ready to learn from any one of good will.

Edward Arbuthnot Knox was his Suffragan. No two men, harnessed together in the common service of the Church, could have differed more in their methods and ideas. Yet Bishop Knox gave him warm-hearted welcome and, directly his appointment to Worcester was announced, referred in the pulpit to the special fitness of the Bishop-designate 'to help those who had lost hold of their Faith under the stress of scientific inquiry.' 'Professor Romanes,' he said, 'a keen Scotsman with all the deep fervour of the Scotsman's faith in God, as a student of science, under the teaching of Darwin and others, lost that faith. By God's mercy and largely through the help of their future Bishop, he recovered that faith before his death.'

There could not well be a more beautiful and moving

testimony from one who might be termed a 'Low Church' Bishop to his Diocesan, a 'High Church' Bishop, than that sent to me by Bishop Knox after Bishop Gore had passed away. I give its conclusion:

He soon found his way to the heart of the city, although he was a high Churchman and the Churchmanship of the city was predominantly Protestant. For Gore, in spite of his Anglican predispositions and his leanings to what is called Modernism, knew what Evangelicalism stood for, and had in his religious composition a strong vein of Evangelicalism. On the vital questions of sin, the Atonement, the need of conversion, and deep reverence for Holy Scripture, Gore was sincerely Evangelical. His teaching was always constructive, not destructive. He began with a course of sermons on the four Gospels, which was on the conservative side, and removed such impression of his heterodoxy as Father Ignatius might have created. The only Confirmation Address which I heard him give was one which I should have been happy to give myself. He conducted a retreat for the Birmingham Clergy, in which the most striking feature was the marvellous use that he made of the Collects, fitting them to his discourses as aptly as if they had been extempore prayers.

During the two years when I served under him as Archdeacon and Bishop Suffragan our relations were as happy as heart could desire. His consideration for me, his determination to consult me, to do nothing without me, have left the happiest recollections. I might almost have been his Bishop and he my Suffragan for the deference that he paid to my wishes and opinions. When he stayed in my house no guest could have been more charming; bubbling over with fun and humour, considerate to the verge of self-effacement, and withal, when work had to be done, tackling it with swift resolution and clear brain, and all the time conscious of the Divine Presence in all his ways, and imparting that consciousness to others. Scholar, theologian, churchman, above all he was a man of God—and there was the secret of his power.

He was loved by working men. In Worcester, they thought and talked of him affectionately as 'Charlie,' and it was in reverence that they did so. This strange aristocrat was one of them. They trusted him. He was their prophet.

A scheme for the division of the unwieldy diocese was initiated by Bishop Philpott in 1889 and abandoned by Bishop Perowne in 1892. In 1903 Gore 'ventured to give a fresh start to the enterprise.' On October

CHARLES GORE AND SIMON IN THE GARDEN OF
MRS. L. C. GREEN-WILKINSON

12th 1904, he was able to say: 'Already we have our money promised and in greater part collected and the necessary Parliamentary facilities provided by the passing of the Southwark and Birmingham Bishopric Bill.' It was a mighty piece of work, largely made possible by the gift of his own patrimony and the generosity of Thomas Henry Freer, Archdeacon of Derby. By December 1904 the division was accomplished, and then, naturally and inevitably, he left the rural part of his old diocese and became first Bishop of Birmingham.

When it was all over he broke down. The old trouble in his eyes, so bad in early days at Westminster, reasserted itself. 'I am not only forbidden to read and write and make public appearances, I am also forbidden to have letters read to me or to dictate answers. I must be allowed to cease to exist until March 2nd 1905.' He welcomed his 'Forty Days.' 'I believe them to have been not without purpose or advantage.'

On March 2nd he was enthroned. In his address, after speaking of the Church of England as 'contributing to the common life side by side with other religious communities,' he said:

When for my own inspiration I think of great Birmingham Christians of the last generation, I think first of two names, neither of them of my own communion—the first a personal spiritual influence of world-wide power and incomparable attractiveness, John Henry Newman; the second, the man who seemed to me to represent ideally the combination of the Christian prophet with the Christian citizen, I mean Robert W. Dale.

Great and passionately loyal Anglican as he was, his relations with members of other religious bodies were almost always happy ones, and with Nonconformists in particular his friendships were many and deep. Joseph Chamberlain often witnessed to Nonconformist feeling for the Bishop, 'who came to Birmingham as a stranger, but now they knew him they could say he had won golden opinions from everybody, from Nonconformists

E

quite as much as Churchmen—and his moderate,
broad, and religious influence had exercised the best
effect on the people of the city.'

For six years he laboured incessantly, preaching,
lecturing, organizing, doing his utmost to encourage
and help any and every effort for social righteousness.
Perhaps he enjoyed most having working men as his
guests. Such occasions as a Co-operative Congress
and an annual gathering of the Workers' Educational
Association gave him special delight.

On the death of Bishop Paget in 1911, Gore, against
his inclination but at the behest of Archbishop Davidson, accepted the See of Oxford. I remember him,
sitting dejectedly in front of the fire at Bishop's Croft
in a characteristic attitude, his head in his hands, saying repeatedly, 'I don't want to go.' Birmingham, on
its part, mourned his going and expressed its appreciation of his work by erecting a statue of him in the
Cathedral Yard. Characteristically, Gore could never
bear to look at it in after years. The statue itself
was unveiled by Archbishop Davidson, who said: 'Dr.
Gore was too great a man for his influence to be confined
to only one Church and one party. The subscribers
included representatives of all classes and all denominations in the city. So the memorial was not only a
Church memorial but a civic one.' Then he continued
humorously: 'I have not yet seen the statue, and I look
forward eagerly to seeing how the artist has reproduced
the characteristics of one whom a would-be sailor boy,
under examination for Osborne, described as a "rather
ragged-looking man."'

There are some who regard his Oxford episcopate as
a misfortune. Yet, who dare criticize it? He had
637 parishes to oversee. He tried gallantly to know
them all. It is true that many of the landowners feared
him, that Oxford University itself shrank from an avowed
reformer, and that country labourers were shy of a
Bishop who longed to walk and to talk with them.
Yet he once again set standards. He toiled unceasingly

at diocesan minutiae. As a 'Father in God' he preached and spoke, he confirmed lovingly.

The working men of Reading discussed whether they should attend a meeting of the Workers' Educational Association at which he was to speak and reluctantly agreed to do so. Ever after they were his captives. They delighted to get him to the Union and Club rooms. A prominent Reading citizen said that in such company the Bishop surpassed himself and was at his happiest.

In agony of mind and spirit he passed through the years of war. His manifest distress throughout was tragic to see.

If it was difficult for him to agree with all the pronouncements of his brother Bishops, yet, while he was on the Bench, he was unswerving in his loyalty to them. To the Archbishop he gave filial obedience. Loyalty to his fellows was an outstanding characteristic of his nature. It is possible that, if by so doing he had not seemed to censure them, he would have lived in a small house as working men lived. Hartlebury, in which he refused to live, and the Palace at Cuddesdon troubled him greatly.

Some have said that the decision not to make Confirmation the condition of admission to the Electoral Roll of the Church of England caused him ultimately to resign. That is, at least, not the whole truth, much as he regretted the decision. He knew that he was not physically and temperamentally able to sustain for much longer the heavy work of his office. Above all, he yearned to make his testimony re-affirming the Faith. His friends encouraged him, and so with this end in view he resigned from his bishopric in 1919 and retired to work in London.

He enjoyed his freedom. In the mornings he wrote, in the afternoons, by lifelong habit, he walked. He made new friends. 'Lame dogs' and young men from King's College, where he had accepted a Lectureship, were always welcome. In the evenings he read everything that he thought mattered. His life was ascetic.

To all that he did in the London years, the books he wrote, the sermons he preached, the lectures he gave, the committees he attended, it is impossible to do justice. In collaboration with the Rev. Dr. A. Guillaume and Canon H. L. Goudge he edited *A New Commentary on Holy Scripture*—a work which by itself might well have taxed the energies of many a younger man. In 1924 he issued his trilogy *The Reconstruction of Belief*, and in 1929 he delivered the Gifford lectures at St. Andrews on *The Philosophy of the Good Life*. He seemed to be more active than ever.

Many came to know him personally for the first time. The Rev. H. A. J. Pearmain writes:

I went to Grosvenor Chapel on the last Sunday in October 1929 and, as we entered, I heard the Litany being read as I had never heard it before. My companion whispered to me, 'It is Bishop Gore.' It was a revelation of 'the beauty of holiness.' It was infinitely more than 'reading prayers'—it was real prayer, rich and deep and true. He seemed to us to consecrate the words in the very uttering of them. Then, at the Sung Eucharist, he preached on 'The Communion of Saints,' remembering All Souls' Tide—with a text from the book of the *Revelation*—and one could almost imagine it was the writer of the *Revelation* himself in that pulpit. He led us to the very brink of the Unseen—some of his words that day I can never forget—towards the end he said: 'You know, we often spend our time deploring "our unhappy divisions." I would remind you that that great Catholic Church which is above (and he looked up to the heavens and spread out those expressive hands) is undivided. If I may say it very reverently, the Church on earth is but, as it were, the lower limbs of the Body of Christ, the Head is above.'

Another, a B.D. student who had Dr. Gore as his tutor at King's College, gives a pleasant glimpse of him there:

As a tutor he was very strict, and required a good deal of hard work from us. At our first talk he told us to go right through the Bible and trace the development of some theological ideas in it. When he marked our fortnightly essays he had evidently gone right through each one thoroughly, and made caustic remarks by word of mouth or on the margin of the essay paper. He would say the most crushing things, but always with a smile, which took all the sting away. He was very keen on our using good English, advising us to read Newman for this purpose. Sometimes, when

CHARLES GORE IN INDIA IN 1931 WITH TWO SONS
OF THE VEN. JOHN GRIMES, ARCHDEACON
OF CALCUTTA

our essays were more absurd than usual, he would talk for half
an hour, sketching in a wonderful forceful way the history of a
people or a religion. He was always very fond of 'dear Zoroaster.'
We always addressed him as 'sir,' which seemed appropriate, as
he always came dressed in a lounge suit and without any Episcopal
adornment. On one occasion he had been very biting in his
comments on my essay, and when we were going, he called me
back and said he hoped that my feelings were not hurt, with many
other kind and encouraging things, ending all with a warm embrace
and his blessing. This typifies our relationship with the Bishop.
He was at once a strict, hard master, and a kind, gentle, fatherly
friend. We felt for him both love and awe.

He was a whole-hearted supporter of the movement
for adult education, both secular and religious. He saw
in Church Tutorial Classes in particular a means of
providing for others that opportunity, which he always
valued for himself, of examining and testing by the light
of reason their grasp and understanding of the Faith.
He was himself one of the founders of the Association,
and remained its Vice-President and constant friend
until his death.

These revelations of a man of seventy years, retired
from high and heavy office, fulfilling an arduous task
with his whole heart and mind, while struggling with
heavy literary tasks, are surely unique in the story of
the Church of England.

Throughout his life he confined his annual holidays
to one month, always spent in travelling, but in 1924
he visited the Near East. 'The main purpose of my
journey,' he wrote, 'was to make myself better acquainted
with the various Orthodox Churches of the Near East,
so as to qualify myself for more effective service on the
Archbishops' Committee for dealing with the Eastern
Churches of which I am Chairman.'

The last great effort of his life was a visit to India.
He was troubled and anxious concerning the South
India scheme. His activity and energy, although he
was in his seventy-eighth year, were unbounded. On
his return he sought to take up the threads of his life
in London, but his strength was failing. He preached

his last sermon in Grosvenor Chapel on September 27th
1931.

On November 20th, he wrote to the Rev. A. Guillaume:

> I am laid by, i.e. my heart collapsed about six weeks ago—India
> having been too much for it—and now I am condemned to total
> abstinence from external activities for six months. I am promised
> complete recovery, but . . .

The week following Christmas he spent at Wool-
beding, the home of his sister, Caroline Lascelles,

where the Christmas party was still assembled, his presence a delight
to young and old. He had his own comfortable sitting-room, so
that he might escape from the noise of young voices and the strident
tones of the gramophone, which now forms a background to every
assembly of youth, but he made little use of it. He enjoyed the
innocent revelry, and his own contribution of humour and gaiety
was priceless. Those privileged to meet him in this, as it proved to
be, the last week of his social life, from the oldest to the youngest,
will cherish this perfect memory of him to their dying day.[1]

On his return he insisted on taking his afternoon
walks, no matter how bitter the wind. So he came to
the last days. Happily, his illness was not protracted.
He passed home on January 22nd 1932.

In the foregoing pages I have attempted, through a
rapid survey of the main events of Charles Gore's life,
to give a picture of a man whose thoughts and actions
will be the subject of many books in the years to come.
He conceived life as 'a deliberate proceeding controlled
by reasonable motives.' In the spirit of this conception
he lived and worked through half a century of development and change in University, Church and State,
striding in power, a commanding figure, across the
stage of England, bearing witness with unflagging
energy to an eternal and unchanging Faith.

No one can understand Charles Gore without realiz-
ing the intense humanity of the man. But it was a
controlled humanity; that impatient, wild, erratic

---

[1] *Church Guardian*, 29th January 1932.

nature of his flickered continuously but never burst into excess. After the first reaction he could bring it under control. It was this humanity which made him so delightful.

It has been said that he was an ascetic by nature, that he 'wore the hair shirt' because he loved it; nothing could be further from the truth. He denied himself and sacrificed much because in no other way could he live the life he had set before him. By nature he was, in the best sense of the word, a worldly man; he had no monastic vocation. Jesus lived in the world, taking part in its pure delights, and so he would live also. He revelled in music, literature, and art. Travel was a never-ending source of joy to him. It was self-evident that his tenderness sprang from, or found its true source in, a constant and loving meditation on the fact of the Incarnation and on the Gospel records. His was a spirit by nature and inheritance wayward, permeated by Grace. 'I am sometimes tempted,' he said, 'to thank God that I am so naturally wicked.'

If he was invited to help, whether in counsel or, we may be sure, in confession, he gave all he had, but he never wantonly invaded the area of any man's mind or soul.

Spiritually he was an optimist, but mentally he was a pessimist. He had no doubts of the final victory, but he found great difficulty in reconciling that great truth with the sorrow and pain of the world.

Yet with all his intense enjoyment of life at many points, there remained a certain aloofness. It is probable that no one knew Charles Gore completely; he seldom talked about himself or his past. Even those who lived with him saw, as it were, only two sides of his life —domestic and public. He drew back into his own retreats, loving intensely silence and quiet in life.

He *was* a saint. He did know how to stand alone; he could stand suspicion and abuse without losing heart or charity. He did know how to hold him fast by God. All this is quite consistent with his having been, probably, mistaken in many details of practice and theory.

For myself, in common with all who knew him intimately, I think of him as one whose conversation was in Heaven.

Nothing small or mean could live in his presence, and if he were stern at times in his treatment of such conduct as he felt obliged to censure in others, he was much sterner with himself. But Charles Gore was not narrow; if he judged a sin as a doctor judges a loathsome disease, he was always tender with those who had sinned. He never judged a man; the recognition of the sacred personality of every man determined all his human relationships.

But, above all else, he was in spirit a little child. As such he entered and lived in the Kingdom of Heaven, having in his strength as a great Christian affected the Church of England more than any other man in his time.

LIKENESS AND DIFFERENCE

I

FOR a proper understanding of Talbot and Gore, of the things which they had in common and of those in which they differed, reference must be made to the state of the Church of England at the time when Talbot at Oxford and Gore at Harrow had determined to serve it to the extent of their powers.

During the previous hundred years three great revivals, the Methodist, the Evangelical, and the Tractarian, had, by their several contributions, enriched the life and practice of the Church of England.

It is difficult at the present time to imagine the state of public worship in the Church of the early nineteenth century. The sacred edifices were often neglected, services were perfunctorily and irregularly held, and pluralism was regarded merely as a sign of skill and success. The beginnings of reform came when Charles Simeon made Holy Trinity Church, Cambridge, the starting point of the Evangelical revival. From that time the same spiritual fervour which had inspired Methodism found new channels for expression within the Anglican Church.

Then came the Tractarian Movement, 'that splendid passage in the history of the national life,' as Lord Haldane called it. It recalled the Church of England to the importance of that fundamental article of her creed which asserts: 'I believe one Catholic and Apostolic Church.' The result of the insistence of the Tractarian leaders on this article of the Creed and all that it involved was to bring about revival in every aspect of the Church's life.

Thus the Church purged herself of many anomalies

71

and rose to a high level of consecrated service in parish
after parish. Slackness diminished, pluralism was prac-
tically abolished, services were regularly and reverently
held. There was manifest vigour. In spite of ritual
disturbances and party strife, the Church deepened
her inner life, and was strengthened to repel new
attacks on her Faith.

The strength and clear vision thus achieved were
plainly needed. New knowledge was in the air.
Scientific discoveries seemed to many to have affected
the authority of the Bible to such an extent as to destroy
the theory of inspiration. Convinced Christians were
faced with the problem of relating their faith to new
scientific statements, at that time no less dogmatic
than their own.

Lyell's *Principles of Geology* was published by 1833, and
Darwin, in 1859, had asserted a theory of Evolution.
His books *The Origin of Species* and *The Descent of Man*
caused widespread disquiet among the orthodox, and
serious questioning among thoughtful people in general.
The New Testament documents had been subjected
to ruthless criticism, notably by eminent German
scholars, led by F. C. Baur in the Tübingen School.
Strauss, who accepted their critical results, was popu-
larized in England by George Eliot, who translated
his *Leben Jesu* in 1846. Renan's *Vie de Jésus* (1863)
exercised in its turn widespread influence among the
general thoughtful public. In spite of the counter-
acting scholarship of Lightfoot, Westcott, and Hort at
Cambridge, and Pusey and Liddon at Oxford, the
general result was a scepticism which invaded the minds
of young men at the Universities. This scepticism was
tempered largely by such men as Thomas Hill Green,
who, unorthodox as he was, had a high conception of
spiritual values.

This was the situation which faced both Talbot and
Gore when, in 1870, Talbot was appointed Warden of
Keble and Gore took up his scholarship at Balliol.
Both of them meditated on these things and deepened

their theological, historical, and philosophical studies until they were equipped, each in his own way, to demonstrate clearly that the new knowledge could be made to minister to the Faith more surely and certainly than to unbelief.

Both of them were deeply influenced by Thomas Hill Green. Scott Holland said : 'He released us from the fear of agnostic mechanism. He gave us back the language of self-sacrifice. We took life from him at its spiritual value.' So many of Green's pupils became leaders in the Church that Mark Pattison, then Rector of Lincoln College, complained humorously that the Churchmen were carrying off Green's honey to their hives.

When Gore was elected a Fellow of Trinity in 1875, Talbot had been Warden of Keble for five years. His influence was exerted not so much by his brilliance as by his faithfulness and humility. He was one of a circle of rather older men, into which Gore describes himself as being drawn, partly as disciple, partly as colleague. As a result of their deliberations they formed what Henry Scott Holland nicknamed 'The Holy Party'—which consisted of men teaching at Oxford between 1875 and 1885, who felt bound by 'disencumbering, re-interpreting, explaining,' 'to attempt to put the Catholic Faith into its right relation to modern intellectual and moral problems.'

It was this group that in 1889 published a volume of Essays under the title *Lux Mundi*, which exercised a profound influence on Christian thought. To this volume Talbot contributed a learned essay in which he gathered up and interpreted the results of criticism in their bearing upon 'The Preparation in History for Christ.' It was a pioneer piece of work.

Gore broke new ground. The Bible was to him the handbook of the living Church. For him it was an inspired creation in which drama and allegory stood out as a means to unfold the revelation of God. Most important of all was his assertion that our Lord, in his human nature, conformed to the limitations of 'perfect man.' He did not bring to bear 'the unveiled omniscience of the Godhead to anticipate or foreclose a development of natural knowledge.' A belief in the Kenosis or 'self-emptying' of Christ was in complete harmony with a right belief in the Incarnation, the eternal and complete Divine Nature expressing itself in and through the terms of temporal human nature which, though perfect, was conditioned in experience and knowledge by the world in which it moved.

After the publication of *Lux Mundi* Talbot pursued his uninterrupted way, but Gore was brought into the fierce light of publicity, and had to bear, brokenheartedly enough, the censure of many of those he loved and respected in the Faith. But he, too, went courageously on.

The group preserved its continuity and met annually for twenty-four years at Longworth Rectory, and then for a few more years at Cuddesdon. Amidst all their work and anxiety Gore and Talbot had always this place of retreat and refreshment.

No more perfect place could have been found for these gatherings than Longworth Rectory, the home of the Rev. and Mrs. J. R. Illingworth. Illingworth himself was a faithful parish priest who 'retired to his quiet parish, and there, loved and honoured, occupied himself in undistracted meditation on God and the world and mankind in the light of the Incarnation: and he gave to the clear vision which he won by meditation singularly lucid and beautiful and convincing expression in a series of books which have had immense circulation, and have been, I should think, more quoted by other philosophical and religious writers than the works of any of his contemporaries.' [1] He provided the group with a philosophical background and to him Gore and Talbot, as well as many of the others, owed much of their inspiration and power. An east

[1] C. Gore, in the Preface to *The Life of John Richardson Illingworth*, by his Wife.

window was erected in the church at Longworth with this inscription:

This window, erected in 1900, was the gift of friends of the Rector, John Richardson Illingworth, who had been fellow-workers with him in the volume entitled *Lux Mundi*, and who year by year met at the Rectory and together joined in the worship of this Church. 'Then they who feared the Lord spake often one to another.'

A list of the members of the first *Lux Mundi* party at Longworth has been preserved. Besides Gore and Talbot, there were present Francis Paget,[1] Walter Lock,[2] Henry Scott Holland, Arthur Lyttelton,[3] R. L. Ottley,[4] R. C. Moberly, and W. J. H. Campion.[5] Henry Scott Holland has delightfully described the Longworth meetings:

We told all the old stories once more that had been a joy of the days which had gone; we repeated all the old jokes that no one knew but we; we laughed once again with the same immemorial laughter that no outsider could understand or share. And then we settled our programme. Five serious subjects were sorted out to fixed hours. Each was allotted to a special member to introduce. Morning and afternoon for three good days we went at it. Gore was our chairman and kept us severely in hand. But there were compensations for the severity in relays of milk and straw-berries, and shouting at meals, and long sittings on the lawn in fine summer days; and walks; and wanderings amid the historic rose gardens; and the unwithering joy of discovering how friend-ships can never weary or lose their immortal freedom. So 'Long-worth' became to us the symbol of all that was deepest in our lives. It acquired a personality of its own. It stood for a certain habit of mind, for an intellectual type, for a spiritual fellowship.[6]

[1] Francis Paget (1851–1911). Senior Student of Christ Church, Oxford 1873–82, Regius Professor of Pastoral Theology at Oxford 1885–92, Dean of Christ Church 1892–1901, Bishop of Oxford 1901–11.
[2] Walter Lock (1846–1933). Fellow of Magdalen, Oxford 1869–92, Warden of Keble 1880–1920, Dean Ireland's Professor of Exegesis 1895–1919, Lady Margaret Professor of Divinity 1919–27.
[3] Arthur Temple Lyttelton (1852–1903). Tutor of Keble, Oxford 1879–82, Master of Selwyn, Cambridge 1882–93, Bishop of Southampton 1898–1903.
[4] Robert Lawrence Ottley (1856–1933). Senior Student of Christ Church, Oxford 1879–96, Vice-Principal of Cuddesdon College 1886–90, Regius Professor of Pastoral Theology 1903–33.
[5] William James Heathcote Campion (1851–92). Tutor of Keble College, Oxford 1882–92.
[6] From an article on John Richardson Illingworth by Henry Scott Holland in *The Commonwealth*.

II

When we turn from the association of Talbot and Gore in the *Lux Mundi* group to a more detailed comparison of their lives, it may be well to begin with an account of the first contact of these two men whose careers were henceforth to run on strangely parallel lines. In a letter written in 1931 Talbot wrote: 'My first recollection of Charles Gore was when I was examining in the School of Honour Greats in 1875, and there I was struck by the uniform excellence of his work. It obtained first class marks throughout, in scholarship, philosophy, and history.' The Bishop remembered no other instance of a first class in every paper. As a result probably of this relationship, the older man developed an attitude towards the younger of proud paternal affection, not unmixed with wonder and awe, which persisted until Gore's death in 1932, two years before Talbot himself died in 1934.

In the procession of great Christians which distinguishes the nineteenth century they walked together, filling the same kind of offices, both in University and Church, and uniting at times in common witness. They appeared as complementary the one to the other to a greater extent than any other two great churchmen of their time. All their speech and actions were in keeping with their untiring witness to the continuing existence in the world of the spiritual body of Christ manifest and revealed in and through the living Church.

Let us glance at the similarities in their careers.

In manners and temper they both revealed their aristocratic lineage. To both it gave entrance to a world which would otherwise have been closed to them but they never allowed it to cut them off from the larger world. They did not reject aristocratic standards and formularies but they expressed whatever in them was good in a setting of natural love of all men, this being, indeed, the very essence of that democratic and international feeling which characterized them.

They derived inspiration from both Evangelicals and Tractarians. Talbot was from the first nurtured in the churchmanship of the Tractarians. Gore was brought up in an Evangelical home but was drawn to the Tractarians by instinctive sympathy while he was still a schoolboy. Both were rooted in the same deep convictions of the Faith and both maintained the same conceptions and practice of the Church based on apostolic foundations and continued in apostolic tradition. There was to them but one final court of appeal, the living Scriptures interpreted by the Church in the power of the Holy Spirit.

They looked with veneration to the same teachers. For scholarship they turned to Lightfoot, Westcott, and Hort. Maurice broadened their conception of the work of Christianity in the world. Both were indelibly affected by the direct influence on them of a group of their early contemporaries, men characterized by high purpose, profound learning and utter consecration of spirit. Merely to think of such men as John Keble,[1] John Henry Newman,[2] Richard William Church,[3] Brooke Foss Westcott,[4] Edward Bouverie Pusey,[5] Henry Parry Liddon, is to have a vision of a torrent of spiritual and intellectual power. To such men both Gore and Talbot owed their development.

Talbot passed from Keble to the Vicarage of Leeds and thence to the See of Rochester. Gore sought parochial experience at Liverpool, became Vice-Principal of Cuddesdon, then Principal Librarian of the Pusey House. After a brief tenure of the Vicarage of

[1] John Keble (1792–1866). Fellow of Oriel, Oxford 1811–23, Professor of Poetry at Oxford 1831–41, Vicar of Hursley 1836–66.

[2] John Henry Newman (1801–90). Fellow of Oriel, Oxford 1822–32, Vicar of St. Mary the Virgin, Oxford 1828–43, entered Roman Church 1845, created Cardinal 1879.

[3] Richard William Church (1815–90). Fellow of Oriel, Oxford 1838–52, Junior Proctor 1844, Dean of St. Paul's 1871–90.

[4] Brooke Foss Westcott (1825–1901). Fellow of Trinity, Cambridge 1849–52, Assistant Master at Harrow 1852–69, Regius Professor of Divinity at Cambridge 1870–90, Canon of Westminster Abbey 1883–90, Bishop of Durham 1890–1901.

[5] Edward Bouverie Pusey (1800–82). Fellow of Oriel, Oxford 1823–8, Regius Professor of Hebrew at Oxford 1828–82.

F

Radley, he went to London as Canon of Westminster almost at the same time as Talbot became Bishop of Rochester, and took up his residence at Kennington. Both attained widespread influence. Gore became a famous expositor, Talbot an inspiring Bishop. They often attended the same meetings, and they collaborated in the work of the Christian Social Union. Their outlook was similar and their witness harmonious. To those who knew them both it was difficult to think of one without the other.

In 1902 Gore became Bishop of Worcester. Both he and Talbot had to face the problem of dividing their respective dioceses. Both succeeded in solving it, and in the same year, 1905, both were translated to city sees which had been created by the same Act of Parliament—Talbot to Southwark, Gore to Birmingham. Strangely enough both were again translated in the same year, Talbot to Winchester and Gore to Oxford in 1911. Both resigned their Bishoprics, Gore retiring in 1919 and Talbot in 1923. Their reasons, however, were different, Gore giving up his Bishopric in order that he might have leisure to write, and Talbot retiring through old age.

Gore's literary output was enormous. He published forty books as well as numerous pamphlets. Talbot's was comparatively small. He made little or no claim to authorship, but was prone to feel that he ought to have written more. Like many others he would have been glad to see evidence of his work on his bookshelves. The difference may be partly accounted for by the fact that Gore was thirteen years younger than Talbot when he retired from office, and that he was free from the duties and responsibilities of family life.

Any one who looks back at the two men in their progress will see that, while Talbot proceeded steadily on his way, contentedly and confidently, stepping little to the right or left, Gore was ever straining at the leash, striving to strike out, to move quickly, though constantly restrained by his unfailing loyalty to his fellow-members of the Anglican Church.

The last years of their lives were spent in retirement. Talbot enjoyed to the full visiting and revisiting the scenes of his former labours in order to cheer and to be cheered by his former colleagues or their successors. His delight was great when he was invited to take part in some function or service.   Gore, on his part, laboured at re-affirming the Faith in books, lectures, and sermons. He was tireless in the work of social reform.   Unlike Talbot he showed little desire to revisit the places where he had worked in former days, but he was always made happy by the visits of those who had worked with him and, as always, was ready to spend and be spent for any one who needed his counsel and help.   He was seldom without a 'lame dog' or two.

III

These two men, each in his own way, and in the power of the Holy Spirit, fulfilled in modern terms the description of 'him that is truly wise' written by Jesus, son of Sirach, over twenty centuries ago:

But he that giveth his mind to the law of the most High, and is occupied in the meditation thereof, will seek out the wisdom of all the ancient, and be occupied in prophecies.

.   .   .   .   .   .

He will give his heart to resort early to the Lord that made him, and will pray before the most High, and will open his mouth in prayer, and make supplication for his sins.

When the great Lord will, he shall be filled with the spirit of understanding; he shall pour out wise sentences, and give thanks unto the Lord in his prayer.

He shall direct his counsel and knowledge, and in his secrets shall he meditate.

He shall show forth that which he hath learned, and shall glory in the law of the covenant of the Lord.

Many shall commend his understanding; and so long as the world endureth, it shall not be blotted out; his memorial shall not depart away, and his name shall live from generation to generation.

Nations shall show forth his wisdom, and the congregation shall declare his praise.[1]

[1] Ecclesiasticus xxxix 1 and 5-10.

Both men were Elizabethan rather than Victorian in type. Their portraits might easily be placed not among the men of their own time but with those of Francis Bacon, Walter Raleigh, or Francis Drake. They embodied the high characteristics and especially the keen, inquisitive vitality which made England great in the sixteenth century.

Neither of them was narrowly puritan. In a real and justifiable sense they were tolerant of the actions of their fellows, in spite of their implacable and unceasing war on sin whether in high or low places. Yet even that war was waged with positive rather than negative weapons. They well knew 'the expulsive power of a new affection.' Their delight was in the beauty and truth of human relationships transformed by the spirit of love. They fulfilled their churchmanship in its breadth, not in its narrowness. Yet both acted definitely and decisively whenever any one in Orders under their jurisdiction was disloyal or publicly impugned the central doctrines of the Church.

Their belief in the apostolic succession determined their conception of the ministry and sacraments of the Church of England. Both, however, learned much from, and were eager to work with, men of other denominations, and both of them acknowledged their indebtedness to the teaching of R. W. Dale, the minister of Carr's Lane Chapel at Birmingham. In their yearning to bring every one into the Church of God, whatever his race, colour, or nation, they strove to hear and to encourage every revelation of knowledge and devotion to be found in other religions or anywhere outside the fold of the Church. It was Talbot who addressed his pastoral letters 'to those who, not of us, yet call upon our Lord Jesus Christ in sincerity and truth,' and Gore who, at Lausanne in 1927, refused to support a resolution until it included due recognition of the light that lighteth every man. In their hearts they yearned for that Church universal which is the 'blessed company of all faithful people.'

EDWARD STUART TALBOT AT STOKE
ROCHFORD
PRESIDING OVER THE ARCHBISHOPS' COMMISSION ON CHRISTIANITY
AND INDUSTRIAL PROBLEMS

From a drawing by the Dean of Westminster

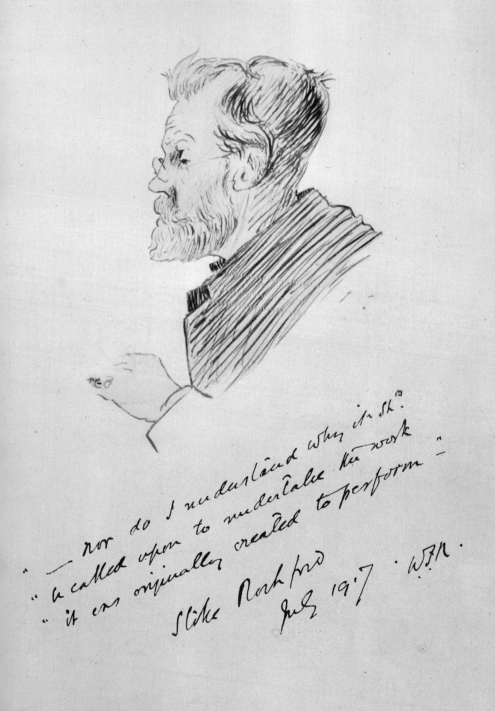

" — nor do I understand why it is." " I is called upon to undertake the work " " it was originally created to perform —"

Slike Rochford
July 1907 · W.F.M.

In breadth of human interest and persistent in-
quisitiveness Talbot surpassed Gore, perhaps because
his life was not passed in such unceasing action. Yet
Gore let little pass him and loved brilliant conversation. His memory was accurate and prodigious. Often
he would burst out with long quotations, verbally correct, from books, novels among them, which he had
read years before.

'WHEN HE COULD STAND NO MORE'
The Bishop of Oxford, 6 p.m. July 28th 1917, at Stoke Rochford.
From a pencil sketch by the Dean of Westminster.

Talbot was more patient than Gore. He could
suffer fools gladly and had not Gore's marked prefer-
ence for brilliant men. In his earlier years Gore re-
acted quickly to undue assertiveness, and he never
quite lost a certain impatience with stupid people.
Many feared him as no one feared Talbot. Yet, para-
doxically enough, one could criticize Gore to his face
in a way in which it would have seemed impertinent
to criticize Bishop Talbot. Both possessed the gift of
humility. In Talbot it was spontaneous, arising out
of a natural simplicity in his nature, while in Gore it
was due to lifelong discipline and constant meditation
on the mind of Christ.

It was easier to know Talbot all round. He intro-
duced his friends to each other but Gore was known
completely to very few people, if any. He was a man of
many parts and kept the parts separate.

Both revelled in social intercourse and in all the

pleasures which delight healthy-minded people. Gore, who never married, was inevitably in after life much more isolated than Talbot and turned to such things as music and art which he could enjoy almost alone. He would have found it boring to watch a cricket match as Talbot loved to do, but then he had no grandson cricketers. Both loved travel, but with Gore it was almost a passion. On his holidays, when he generally had a friend or a niece for companion, he revelled in new scenes and experiences.

It was a joy to both of them to visit the homes of their friends. To Gore especially who had no family life of his own these contacts meant very much. In spirit he shared the happiness which he perceived in the lives of those whom he married, rejoicing greatly when, as sometimes happened, he was able in due time to marry the second generation. In their children he took a fatherly delight. He never forgot them. Perhaps the happiest moments of his life were when he found little ones to play with, whether in the city streets, the lanes at Cuddesdon, or in the homes he visited. Talbot loved children too, but it is doubtful if he would have stopped as Gore once did, outside the Houses of Parliament, in apron, gaiters and all, to join some little boys playing in a roadside sand-bin. Moreover, for Talbot there were his own children and his grandchildren to whom he was ever a loved and delightful companion, knowing how to play their games in their way.

There was no trace of priggishness in either of them. They were delightfully human. An Australian Bishop made them rock with laughter as he told them stories in the vernacular of the back-blocks. In a country house, during a week-end meeting of the Archbishops' Commission on Industrial Relations of which Talbot was Chairman, some daring younger members, in an interval of recreation, tried Bishop Talbot out by giving him some of Calverley's poems to read aloud. Without hesitation he trumpeted out every word with gusto and some were certainly unfamiliar. Gore, who was also present, may have been a little envious; he certainly enjoyed the fun of it. Both of them loved the laughter and joy of human fellowship. Since in these lectures we have been chiefly considering their continuous witness to and interpretation of the Faith in Church and State, it is, perhaps, fitting that our last glimpse of them should be in so human a setting.

EPILOGUE

In every generation one of the chief sources of encouragement to those who would wish to play their part as torch-bearers in the race is to be found in the achievements of those who have carried the torch thus far. Many of us to-day feel that we received it from Edward Talbot and Charles Gore. The preceding pages have brought out vividly and, I believe, truthfully the striking differences between these men who throughout their lives were colleagues in the service of one cause.

Gore was the more dramatic figure — a veritable prophet of social righteousness who found the sustaining inspiration for his challenges to the world in an intensely held and clearly formulated faith. He knew quite well that many of his convictions were held on a balance of evidence, but he held these with as full an assurance as if there were no contrary case to be considered. He had struck the balance and formed his judgment. This gave him immense energy in utterance and in action. He knew precisely where he stood. And those who responded to his call rallied round him as a standard-bearer. His intellect was powerful and penetrating, and could have been used for philosophical work of a high order. But he had not the temperament of a philosopher. He was not greatly interested in the process of arriving at convictions; it was the convictions themselves that concerned him. He had a passion for truth, and subjected his beliefs to rigorous criticism; yet interest was always centred upon the beliefs themselves, and upon the validity of the reasoning behind them only as this affected the beliefs. Thus in his Gifford Lectures he dealt with the problem of

Free Will by assuring us that after long and careful reflection he was convinced of the reality of freedom; what was the actual course of the reflection—the point most interesting to a philosopher—he did not disclose.

Perhaps it is characteristic, or, rather, illustrative of his character, that he was brought up an Evangelical and became a 'Catholic' in conscious re-action. There was here some resemblance to the spiritual development of Newman. Talbot, on the other hand, resembled Keble in that he was brought up as a High Churchman and never varied his central position though he greatly extended his horizon. In other ways also he was the opposite and complement of Gore. He seldom had a well defined position upon a controversial issue. There might be no doubt on which side of a dividing line his chief sympathies lay, but he remained vividly aware of the case for other opinions. Thus he was not so effective a leader to those who initially agreed with him; but he was far more effective in winning acquiescence or even assent from those who initially disagreed. It was clear to all that at every stage he was thinking through once more the subject under discussion, even welcoming new considerations which called for a complete review of convictions long cherished. He was essentially more liberal-minded than Gore, though less associated in the public mind with opinions of the kind called liberal. He was less of a prophet and of more philosophical temperament, though his religion was less intellectualized.

Diverse as were the temperaments of the two men, their varying gifts were controlled by a common devotion. Each in the depths of his soul was dedicated to Jesus Christ as Lord and God; each found this dedication to involve a living sense of the Catholic Church as a fellowship wherein all barriers of date and place are abolished; and each felt himself called, so far as in him lay, to make that fellowship a source of constant influence in the general life of men, moulding it according to the principles of the Gospel in which the fellowship is grounded and of which it is itself an expression. So they laboured together for Liberal Catholicism and for Christian Socialism, supplementing one another's service to the common cause through the diversity of their natural qualities.

In both there was a singular simplicity and a singular depth; but the circumstances that revealed these qualities were different. I used to think that no one really knew Gore who had not both heard him preach a devotional sermon and played golf-croquet with him—activities at the two extremes of the scale of seriousness; while to know Talbot the necessities were to watch him when engaged in discussion with quite young and inexperienced men (especially if one were one of these) and to hear him read the Bible at family prayers. Gore had more of fierce passion and light-hearted frivolity; Talbot more of steady glow and constant kindliness. Gore's mind asked more questions but was restless till they were answered; Talbot rather brooded over the subject and was content that much should be as yet indeterminate. Gore told me once that he regarded St. John as a foreign country which it is a delight to visit, but as he turned to St. Paul he had the sensation of coming home. I never heard Talbot express himself on that matter, but I suspect that he would have found it hard to attach himself to either rather than the other, but if pressed would have ranged himself with St. John.

The Church which gives birth to two such men in a generation—and we recall with them their friends and contemporaries, Scott Holland, Illingworth and the rest—and which holds their loyalty and uses their diverse gifts, declares thereby that the blessing of God is upon it and gains therefrom yet richer blessing.

October 1934.